Life on a Roller Coaster

Coping with the Ups and Downs of Mood Disorders

Ekkehard Othmer, M.D., Ph.D.
and
Sieglinde C. Othmer, Ph.D.

This book is not intended to replace personal medical care and supervision; there is no substitute for the experience and information that your doctor can provide. Rather, it is our hope that this book will provide additional information to help people understand the complex issues of manic-depressive disorder.

Proper medical care should always be tailored to the individual patient. If you read something in this book that seems to conflict with your doctor's instructions, contact your doctor. Your doctor may have medically sound reasons for recommending treatment that may differ from the information presented in this book.

If you have any questions about any treatment in this book, consult your doctor.

In addition, the patient names and cases used in this book do not represent actual people, but are composite cases drawn from several sources.

Other PIA Press Books

The Good News About Depression, by Mark S. Gold, M.D.

The Good News About Panic, Anxiety and Phobias, by Mark S. Gold, M.D.

Sixty Ways to Make Stress Work for You, by Andrew E. Slaby, M.D., Ph.D., M.P.H.

Guide To The New Medicines Of The Mind, by Jeffrey L. Berlant, M.D., Ph.D., Irl Extein, M.D., Larry S. Kirstein, M.D.

The Facts About Drugs and Alcohol, 3rd edition, by Mark S. Gold, M.D.

Get Smart About Weight Control, by Phillip M. Sinaikin, M.D.

High Times/Low Times: The Many Faces of Adolescent Depression, by John E. Meeks, M.D.

Kids Who Do/Kids Who Don't: A Parent's Guide to Teens and Drugs, by Lorraine Hendricks, M.D.

On the Edge: The Love/Hate World of the Borderline Personality, by Neil D. Price, M.D.

Overcoming Insomnia, by Donald R. Sweeney, M.D., Ph.D.

When Acting Out Isn't Acting: Understanding Child and Adolescent Temper, Anger and Behavior Disorders, by Lynne W. Weisberg, M.D., Ph.D. and Rosalie Greenberg, M.D.

800 COCAINE, by Mark S. Gold, M.D.

Light Up Your Blues: Understanding and Overcoming Seasonal Affective Disorders, by Robert N. Moreines, M.D. and Patricia L. McGuire, M.D.

A Parent's Guide to Common and Uncommon School Problems, by David A. Gross, M.D. and Irl L. Extein, M.D.

Aftershock, by Andrew E. Slaby, M.D., Ph.D., M.P.H.

A Consumer's Guide to Psychiatric Diagnosis, by Mark A. Gould, M.D.

Kids Out of Control, by Alan M. Cohen, M.D.

Psychiatric Skeletons: Tracing the Legacy of Mental Illness in the Family, by Steven D. Targum, M.D.

Table Of Contents

DEDICATION

To Our Patients
and
Their Families

ACKNOWLEDGMENTS

Our thanks go first to the staff of PIA Press, headed by Larry Chilnick, who convinced us to pursue a general-audience book; and to Dan Montopoli, Rochelle Ratner, and Janet Chilnick, who assisted in drafting the text and oversaw editorial details.

Second, we thank Norm Zober, Bill Vickers, Ron Bernstein, and Tom Trenary of PIA (Psychiatric Institutes of America) for their organizational support.

Third, we thank our son, Philipp J. Othmer, English and Philosophy major at Vanderbilt University, and presently intern at the American Psychiatric Press, for his editorial input.

And here is our special thank you, Bill McKnelly, M.D., for coming through again. You are one of the pioneers in the treatment of manic-depressive disorder in this country, one of the first to use lithium. You helped us with your support.

Chapter 1

Living the Roller Coaster Life

ROLLER COASTER MOOD

Roller coasters are fun. They're meant to be. The ride lasts only a few minutes, and people pay to get on. However, there's one kind of roller coaster people would pay to get *off*: the wild ride of manic-depressive disorder. Imagine boarding a roller coaster in California and being strapped in all the way to Connecticut—or beyond. Without treatment, your ride might last a lifetime.

The highs on this emotional roller coaster are called manic episodes. They're times of irrepressible optimism, times of feeling great, times when anything is possible. Hurdles look like opportunities; mountains seem like molehills. Everyone is worth meeting. Fun is spelled out in capital letters. Mania means you're the life of the party, with back-slapping enthusiasm.

1

So what's the problem? Mania sounds great.

No, mania has its down side. Sure, everyone enjoys the manic person for a few hours. But then this human sparkplug becomes intrusive, domineering, and demanding. He* speaks too loud and too fast; he jokes, puns, rhymes, and switches from topic to topic. He refuses to take no for an answer. The fun guy turns into a pain in the neck. People wish he'd get lost. In addition, his judgment is impaired. Maybe he spends his life savings on lottery tickets, sure that the big jackpot is coming his way. He can wreak financial ruin on himself and his family in a few impulsive minutes.

Then he hits the low end: depression. Nothing can get him out of the doldrums. Everything looks bleak. He has no energy to do anything. He skips work—the thought of spending the day there is unbearable. Death may look like a welcome relief. Why not jump off the roller coaster? Suicide, yes, that's what it will take to stop this crazy ride.

INSIDE THE ROLLER COASTER:
JACQUELINE'S STORY†

"Peanut butter and jelly sandwiches, yeah, that's what I'll feed the kids tonight. Damn you, Timmy, if you bitch about peanut butter you can stick it! That's all I can take tonight, huh. Huh, am I getting hot again.

Hey mister, go, go . . . For God's sake, the light's not getting any greener. I'll show you! Honk, honk, honk . . . *These assholes don't know how to drive. They just like*

---

*Note: Although this book concerns both male and female patients and therapists, the male pronoun will be used as a matter of convenience.
†All patient names and their identifying characteristics have been changed to protect patient privacy.

to hang around an intersection. I would never date a guy like that. I'll bump that idiot! Damn that Howard. I've told him a thousand times I need to get out of that office by ten to five. I don't want to get stuck in traffic. Why the hell does he always want to talk, talk, talk? He damn well knows I want to run. I bet he does it on purpose, that S.O.B. But I'll show him ...yeah, it's already twenty after. I'll be late at the doctor's. He'll be pissed off.

Dennis ...what a riot ...my kid's father, damn it, you'd think he'd give a damn. I got it all wrong. Idiot, I thought when we split up it would be better for everyone. He'd spend some time with these kids finally. They don't need a father who's always busy with his crap. Sales over souls, American business, right? Macaroni and cheese, yeah, they'll like that better, Timmy and Jason both do. I shouldn't take it out on them just 'cause I'm wired. Am I getting high again? Nah, not over the edge yet, I can still catch myself. Stop, stop, stop ...stop it. Huh!

This jerk in front of me won't move again. He's slow, really slow. Must be having one of his down days—is he depressed? When I'm like that I have to drag myself out of bed. Never get a damn thing done. Someone has to push me.

'Do you want me to go on, Doc?'

'Since you're at it, Jacqueline, it really helps. Trying to remember your self-talk gives me a feel for what mood you're in—how quickly it changes.'

'Okay, here's some more of it. I honked a lot because I didn't want to be late. This idiot was just in front of me. He always stopped on yellow. Couldn't push himself through.'

'Just try to relive it, Jacqueline.'

'Okay, Doc.'

Come on, you can do it. I can feel it already, this is going to be one of those nights. The kids will do nothing but play with their food. It'll drive me nuts.

Keep your cool, Jacqueline. You deal with clients all day long. It's a mystery how I do it. But it's not as easy as it used to be, that's for sure. I was such a professional, but not anymore. I'm not coping, no matter what they say. They don't know what's going on inside me, they don't know my ups and downs have taken over.

My pen? I have to call my lawyer tomorrow. I better make myself a note. Writing while driving, real safe.

What the hell's taking that guy so long? A simple divorce, uncontested, joint custody. Should have been final months ago. I'm not getting any younger—33 years old looking like 29. Let's go for it, as long as Lou is taken by my auburn mane. Maybe just screw it all? Just go back with Dennis. I'll say one thing, I couldn't stand Lou tonight. When I'm high, he's lots of fun. Monday was great. What a good f—k, and then over to his friend's for the double whammy. But not tonight. I can't hack it. Can't push myself any more tonight. Lou's no better for me than Dennis is, just different, that's all. I know, I know. I wonder, why the hell do I push for divorce? The kids need a father, no question about it. But Dennis? They may as well go out in the yard and build a snowman for a father.

'That was my last thought just out there in the parking lot before I came into your office.'"

Later, Jacqueline tells me, "I'm living on that roller coaster you talked about—day in, day out."

Most of us can remember being on a roller coaster ride. Maybe it was wonderful at the time. Remember walking along the ramp... the merry-go-round muddles through its melodies... the cotton candy smell... you squeeze into the roller coaster car. The attendant clamps the seat belt tightly over your lap. Then, jerks and jolts. Uphill. Slowly. The car stalls. Will it ever make the climb? Then, *whoosshhhh*, downhill full speed, hair flying. Laughter and shrieking, screams fill the air. Are those really your screams? And up and down and up and down again. After a few minutes— though it seems like hours—the ride is over. You walk down the ramp, exhilarated, wobbly legs relearning their movements. Maybe you feel dizzy and sick, and decide this was your last ride. Or maybe you're already yearning for the next summer's fun.

But how would it feel to live like Jacqueline—endlessly riding a roller coaster, with no time to regain emotional balance between dizzying heights and stomach-dropping plunges?

Family and friends are often the first ones to notice: "What is it with her? Always up or down, real roller coaster moods."

OUTSIDE THE ROLLER COASTER: JOYCE'S BROTHER'S STORY

"You've got to help my sister, Doc. For the past month she's been lying on her bed, doesn't want to eat, doesn't sleep much, doesn't talk. We knock on the door and she tells us to leave her alone.

We called her doctor at the hospital where she was last time, and he said she may need shock treatments if the medications don't work. But I don't know. I can't see putting her through that again. She's had them three times before, and sure enough she got better. But she'll be seventy-three years old next month—isn't that too old for all those shocks? They tried lithium, but she's not taking it. Says it makes her gain weight.

She still thinks she's going to catch herself another husband. The last two divorced her, they couldn't take her moods.

Most of her life she's been up for a few months, then all the way down. Down in July and August, right before her birthday, like now.

Before this, last May, she calls me up and says she's getting married tonight. Someone she met at the bridge club, his wife died two months ago. How long has she known him? Just today. Seventy-two years old and she's going to get married to a man she met this afternoon. I called her doctor. He doped her up so much, she didn't know up from down. The guy? What did she care. Once she came out of her sleep she didn't even give him a second thought.

Then just last year, again, at the housing complex where she lives. Nice houses, built for seniors, no steps, people who come to mow the lawns, a golf course in the complex, refined, good people. Tired people, like my wife and me. Joyce appoints herself "entertainment coordinator." Starts planning picnics, card games, even a tennis tournament, going up and down the blocks ringing doorbells and getting people to join in, calling them old fuddy duddies when they refuse.

As soon as I saw her I knew she was headed for a down again. Finally she crashed, sat alone in the house, wouldn't answer the phone. You could see from the weight she lost that she wasn't eating. That's when we took her to our house for a while; we thought maybe it would help her to have people around all the time. But she's not getting any better, and we can't take it any longer. That's why we brought her here."

The endless roller coaster mood can affect people at any age, whether seventy or seven. Meet seven-year-old Kevin. Since he has seen his mother's mood swings, he has good insight into his own condition.

INSIDE THE ROLLER COASTER: KEVIN'S STORY

"Three plus three is eight. I should draw my numbers big, fill all the spaces between the two lines, all the way. Don't want her to yell at me again. Sloppy, sloppy, sloppy, Kevin. Gosh. Three plus three? . . . is eight? No, wrong! Bonkers! Three plus three is . . . Why try? Even if I make 'em good it's not gonna be right. I never do anything right. (He starts crying.)

We switched places again yesterday, two tables together, then one by itself. Guess who's sitting alone. It's always me. I end up alone. I'll always be alone. (Sobbing.) *"It's all just inside me, like that monster in Alien: I feel so sad. I feel sad for no reason. I cry but I don't know why. It wasn't like I fell down and hurt myself. Joe didn't even make fun of me or anything. I'm just sitting there crying for no reason.*

When I get excited it's the same way, I don't know

*why, I'm just laughing or yelling. I'm just hyper, three
and three is six, that's it, big deal, what does it matter
anyway? All I want to do is cry, but I can't. I can't do it
like other kids can. What's wrong with me?"*

WHY ISN'T EVERYONE ON SOLID GROUND?

In recent years, research has shown that many people who
suffer from ups and downs have a biochemical imbalance that
we can control with the proper medications. Ask Jacqueline,
or Joyce, or Kevin. For all three of them, as we'll see later,
life improved dramatically when they received medication.
With appropriate therapy, up to 80 percent of patients
with manic-depressive disorder—or just mood swings—can
be relatively free of symptoms, and another 17 percent can
bring their condition under some control. However, the
remaining 3 percent are tough to treat.

If you have strep throat, you take antibiotics to kill the
streptococcus bacillus. And if your daughter falls down and
breaks her arm, you take her to a medical doctor to have it
put in a cast.

Now, imagine your reaction if the doctor examined your
daughter and told you what inner conflicts had caused her to
fall down and break her arm. You'd either be outraged or
amused. You'd say, "But what about the fracture?"

This analogy isn't as far-fetched as you may think. People who
suffer from biochemical imbalances in the brain can be like the
girl with the broken arm. They may spend years and small for-
tunes on psychotherapy, trying to discover the hidden conflicts
that supposedly cause them to feel so depressed or moody. This
amounts to treating the mental pain related to the chemical
imbalance, but not the imbalance itself. True, such psychotherapy may give the patient far better insights into himself.

But it can't change the actual mood disturbance any better than it could have healed that child's broken arm.

THE RIGHT STUFF

As medical director of North Hills Hospital in Kansas City, Missouri, I see firsthand the devastating effects of life on the roller coaster. I have seen patients in their manic highs, in their deep depressions, and in between as they struggle to balance the peaks and valleys of the personal roller coaster. And I have met with hundreds of bewildered family members, who often feel like hostages, strapped into their relative's roller coaster.

In this book, we offer some guidelines to the signs and symptoms of the chemical imbalance that can turn a person's life into an emotional roller coaster.

We explain what psychiatrists look for when they perform various tests, and we point out things you should tell your doctor. We explore the genetic studies that try to clarify how mood disorders may be transmitted from parent to child. We also discuss how stress affects mood swings. We discuss various forms of treatment—treatment by psychiatrists, psychologists, and social workers. Finally, we show you how you can better understand yourself, and thus soften the impact of mood swings you may experience.

This book has a message:

Biochemical imbalance is nobody's "fault." There's no reason to blame your parents for the way they raised you, and there's no reason to blame yourself that you have failed to deal adequately with stress. Furthermore, there is hope—lots of hope—for help.

EXPERTISE AND EXPERIENCE

In my years of treating patients with mood swings, first as a Ph.D. psychologist and later as an M.D. specializing in psychiatry, I have learned the importance of combining psychotherapy with the solid, biologically based approach of modern medical psychiatry. This approach uses medical procedures with the latest advances in diagnostic and therapeutic techniques.

Progress is being made continuously. As mental health professionals, we have to keep up with that progress.

My wife, Sieglinde, a social scientist and research assistant professor of psychiatry at the University of Kansas Medical Center, is at the forefront of that progress. She is working on investigative studies on compounds that have not yet been approved by the Food and Drug Administration, but which might lead to a breakthrough in treating bipolar, or manic-depressive, disorder and depression. Together we study what may be the new generation "wonder drugs," such as adinazolam, aza-mianserin, bupropion, and others.

Husband and wife, we have worked both together and alone. This book reflects some of our results. We describe the biochemical basis of emotional disorders, where our work intertwines. We also write about the symptoms that chemical imbalances cause, and the resulting interpersonal conflicts—from infancy to the senior years—that shape the lives of patients born with a predisposition to mood swings.

ROLLER COASTER SPEEDS AND SIZES

The perpetual roller coasters of life come in different forms and sizes, and are called by different names. An emotional roller coaster with small-to-medium ups and downs might be called *mood swings,* or just plain moodiness. Psychiatric patients on a bigger ride, with higher ups and lower downs, often say they have *manic-depressive* illness. Clinicians say these patients have *bipolar disorder.* They make further distinctions, too, describing bipolar I and bipolar II disorder; some even recognize bipolar disorders III, IV, V, and VI. Let's take a moment to define a few useful clinical terms.

Affective Disorder

This blanket term for any mood disorder applies both to manic-depressive illness and to depression alone. Most affective disorders are caused by biochemical imbalances in the brain, rather than by conflicts within the psyche.

This by no means implies that the chemically imbalanced person is free from conflicts. But it's the old question of which came first, the chicken or the egg? For example, when a woman feels down, she may point to an event that supposedly caused her low mood: the loss of a job, the death of an acquaintance, or simply the lack of a date on Saturday night. Often, however, this is just a "made-up" reason—a seemingly plausible explanation for a hard-to-understand emotional state. Depression has a vacuum-cleaner effect, sucking up "dirt" (mishaps that might befall anyone) and using it as principal thought content. In fact, a biochemical imbalance may lie at the root of this woman's uncomfortable mood.

Cyclothymia

People with cyclothymia suffer from both depressive and manic moods, but both tend to be *mild*—not too low and not too high. During a down, they can't work up energy to move. During a manic period, they can't sit still. Their chief complaint might be that they are always either up or down; they don't tend to stay in the normal range for very long.

Rapid Cyclers

In contrast to people with cyclothymia, rapid cyclers have *severe* symptoms of both mania and depression; they switch quickly from one state to the other. Jacqueline, at the start of this chapter, is a rapid cycler; we'll explore her symptoms more thoroughly in Chapter Seven.

Bipolar

This adjective literally means "having two poles." In manic-depressive disorder, the opposing emotional poles are mania and depression. Most people whose moods swing widely from pole to pole also have periods where they feel somewhere in the middle—i.e., normal. During a high or a low, they have diminished insight into their mood; they tend not to recognize that they're at an emotional extreme. It's during the normal times that they can stand back, take a look at themselves, and realize how unusual their previous behaviors were.

Bipolar I (Manic-Depressive) Disorder

What most people think of as manic-depressive disorder—alternating periods of severe mania and severe depression—is what clinicians call *bipolar I disorder*. Both the extreme highs and the extreme lows of this condition may require hospitalization. The in-between normal feeling is called *euthymic* mood.

Contrary to popular belief, manic-depressive cycles are rarely balanced. A bipolar I person might stay in the normal state for years before having a bout of severe, incapacitating, perhaps suicidal depression. After that he might experience a stable period again, and then enter either a devastating manic phase or another round of depression. Both the depressions and the manic periods are quite noticeable to the people around him. Families prefer to live with the patient, when he is depressed, but the patient himself mostly prefers the highs.

Usually the patient himself notices his depressed mood, but blames it on stress in his life. He may also feel intense guilt and believe, contrary to evidence, that he has committed a sin or a crime. This false belief may be so firmly fixed in his mind that no amount of reasoning can shake it. Such a fixed false belief is called a *delusion*.

During mania, too, the bipolar I person may suffer from delusions—especially delusions of grandeur, which cause him to feel he has unlimited power to save the world. "Crazy" ideas of this type sometimes lead to a misdiagnosis of schizophrenia.

Depressed phases tend to last longer than manic phases. Men may experience mania more often than women, while women are more prone to depressed periods.

Bipolar II Disorder

Patients with this condition suffer from severe depressions that may require hospitalization, as in bipolar I disorder. Their manic phases, however, are mild enough to merit the special name of *hypomania*. During a hypomanic phase the person is highly energized and feels in an unusually good mood, although sometimes it's more of an irritable mood. She may sit down and write hundreds of letters, call friends she hasn't seen in years, or stay up all night cleaning the house. Because she feels so good about herself, her judgment is mildly impaired. She's prone to impulsive decisions, some of which may have serious repercussions.

Bipolar Spectrum

Some psychiatrists believe there is a spectrum of bipolar disorders. For instance, one system breaks the spectrum into six bands:

Bipolar I: Both major depression and mania.

Bipolar II: Major depression alternating with hypomania (a less severe form of mania).

Bipolar III: Cyclothymia, as previously described: mild depression alternating with hypomania. In the past, this was considered a personality disorder.

Bipolar IV: Depression and, usually, no mania; however, certain antidepressant medications can trigger mania.

Bipolar V: Depression and no mania—but some blood relatives have had manic episodes. For bipolar V patients, the best medication for depression may be the one that works for their manic-depressive relatives.

Bipolar VI: Mania and no depression—a very rare condition. The justification for classifying this syndrome among the bipolar ("two-poled") disorders is the belief that almost every manic person will sooner or later crash into a depressive episode.

* * *

Now that we've defined our terms, we're ready to address an issue that may be troubling you: "Do I, or does someone I know, suffer from mood swings? Are these mood swings serious enough that they might call for treatment—or eventually, hospitalization?"

Chapter 2

Do I Suffer From the Roller Coaster Life?

LOOKING BACK AT THE ROLLER COASTER: BRENDA

"I remember one time, years ago, when I went downstairs because I couldn't sleep. Suddenly I couldn't stand the living room another minute. Just looking at it got me into a rage. So I moved stuff around—sofa, chairs, tables, bookcases. Moved them one way, then another, then back again. I changed that room around and around. Three o'clock in the morning and I'm moving furniture!

My husband came downstairs and screamed, 'Stop it! Stop it! Are you nuts? What's got into you?' My mind was going a mile a minute, and I screamed something back at him. He yelled, 'Shut up, motor mouth!' And then he called my doctor, right then in the middle of the night."

All of us have experienced moments of excitement and increased activity. But most of us have never rearranged the furniture at three A.M.

What about lows?

"Ten days later, I'm lying in my hospital bed. 'Don't you want to get up?' asks the nurse on the morning shift. I just look at her and don't move. My psychiatrist comes back for his morning rounds. The nurse asks him, 'Shall we make her get up, doc?' I hear him say, 'There's no use; let her be. She just plunged from her high to her low. She has severe mood swings."

All of us have had low days, but few of us have spent whole days feeling paralyzed, unable to get out of bed, unwilling to talk, not wanting to eat or, for that matter, to live. Most of us don't suffer from severe mood swings.

How do you judge whether a mood swing is severe? Since people often don't recognize their own mood swings, we're going to list a few questions that form a self-test. These questions have been tried many times and found to work; they're part of a standard procedure called the psychiatric diagnostic interview.

Of course, a self-test is just a screening tool. It can't replace a physician's complete assessment. Nevertheless, the answers you give may suggest a need for psychiatric help.

Take a little time with your answers, and be honest with yourself. There are no right or wrong answers—no one is grading you on how good or bad a person you are.

SELF-TEST FOR MAJOR DEPRESSIVE
MOOD SWINGS

1. Have there ever been times when you felt unusually depressed, empty, sad, or hopeless for several days or weeks at a time?
2. Have there ever been times when you felt very irritable or tired most of the time for hardly any reason at all?
3. (If yes on item 1 or 2) How long do these feelings usually last? Have these feelings ever stayed with you most of the time for as long as two weeks?

SELF-TEST FOR MANIC MOOD SWINGS

1. Have there ever been times when you felt unusually high, charged up, excited, or restless for several days at a time?
2. Have there ever been times when other people said that you were too high, too charged up, too excited, or too talkative?
3. How long do these mood changes usually last? Have these high, excitable moods ever stayed with you most of the time for at least a few days?

A KEY TO THE QUESTIONS

If you answered yes to either question 1 or 2 *and* question 3, for major depression *or* mania, it's likely you suffer from at least mild depressive or manic mood swings, or both.

To decide whether you have a depressive or manic-depressive disorder that may require treatment, try answering the following eight questions. They measure the impact mood swings have on your life.

1. Have mood changes ever interfered with your school, your work, or your job?
2. Have your mood changes ever caused any problems with your family, or caused your family to worry about you?
3. Have mood changes ever interfered with your social activities or friendships?
4. Have you ever gotten into trouble with the authorities because of your excited mood?
5. Were you ever so depressed that you thought seriously about taking your own life?
6. Have you ever received medication or treatment for your mood swings?
7. Were you ever hospitalized for mood swings?
8. When you had mood swings, were you unable to take care of yourself?

These eight questions assess your level of functioning. If you answered yes to even one of them, there's about a 90 percent chance you meet the criteria for major depression or manic-depressive disorder.

Since you may still be uncertain, we'll now list a few more questions—six for major depression and another six for mania. In either category, if you answer yes to one of the first two questions *and* to one of questions 3 to 6, you may indeed have a mood disorder. If your mood problems lasted for more than a week, and interfered with your life, you may want to consult a professional.

Self-Test for Depression

1. Have you ever suffered from a prolonged, inexplicable lack of energy?
2. Have you ever found yourself unable to get interested in things you usually enjoy?
3. Was there ever a time when you began losing weight without dieting or exercising strenuously?
4. Did you ever have long periods where you did not want to eat?
5. Do you often feel restless or have trouble concentrating?
6. Have you ever gone through a period where you consistently woke up too early, tossed and turned, and could not go back to sleep?

Self-Test for Mania

1. Did people ever accuse you of being high when you knew you were not?
2. Did you ever start more projects than you could finish, or overload yourself with responsibilities?
3. Did you ever stay up all night, busy writing letters, cleaning the house, or doing work that could easily wait?
4. Have you ever been through a period where you needed almost no sleep?
5. Have you ever been on a spending spree and wasted large amounts of money?
6. Were there ever times when you made a fool of yourself in public by silly talk and clowning?

If your answers to these self-tests suggest that you have a mood disorder, it's time to seek an expert opinion! Remember, symptoms of depression or mania become significant *as soon as they interfere with your ability to function*.

There is also a three-alarm symptom that's in a class by itself. If you've ever made a serious plan to kill yourself by shooting, hanging, jumping from a high building, or any other quick and irreversible means, *take this very seriously*. *DO NOT FAIL TO GET PSYCHIATRIC HELP!*

CREATIVE COMPANY

The person with manic-depressive disorder may be a valuable asset to society. Some of our finest writers and artists have been manic-depressive. For example, Ludwig van Beethoven, Charles Dickens, Vincent Van Gogh, and Ernest Hemingway all suffered from this condition. During his manic periods, when he wanted to catch light, Van Gogh painted fireballs—an apt theme for mania. When he was depressed he'd paint black crows over a wheat field, or a skull smoking a cigarette.

Manic-depressive writers and artists who feel intensely creative when they're high may later regret their lack of discrimination. When they're depressed—provided the depression isn't paralyzing—their creativity may take the form of critical insight to revise and refine the original "raw" work.

MAJOR DEPRESSION: THE OUTCOME

The more depressed you get, the more hopeless you feel, and this hopelessness is devastating. You may feel so miserable that you're certain you'll soon be dead. You can't remember what it's like not to be down. Left untreated, the black cloud may hover over you for months.

Although most depressions go away by themselves after eight to nine months, some manic-depressive patients have reported depressions lasting two years or longer.

Our advice is: Don't "wait out" a depression. Don't suffer unnecessarily. Effective treatments are available.

MANIC-DEPRESSIVE ILLNESS: THE OUTCOME

Whereas depression brings hopeless, suicidal feelings, mania makes you feel angry, impatient, or grandiose. You're driven to assert yourself, to expand. You strive to experience life to the fullest, even to the point of self-destruction. You're like the boy Icarus in the Greek myth, who was so overjoyed with his artificial wings that he flew nearer and nearer to the sun, finally crashing to earth when the sun's heat melted the wax in his wings.

Unlike major depression, which generally has a 70 percent recurrence rate, the double tragedy of manic-depressive illness can often be *controlled indefinitely* with a medication called lithium. This substance is a naturally occurring salt; one of my patients calls it "the salt of the earth."

How can a psychiatrist tell whether your mood swings are caused by major depression or by manic-depressive illness? There are two important areas of inquiry to help distinguish between the two: the course of your own illness, and any history of psychiatric illness in your family.

TRACKING THE COURSE

How old were you when depression or mania first struck?
Bipolar disorder often begins in adolescence and young adulthood, whereas depression may make its first appearance in middle age. In teenagers, mild to moderate symptoms of both depression and mania frequently go undiagnosed. Think carefully before you answer these questions. Can you remember a time when you felt upset and irritable for weeks, so that your whole family was drawn into your mood?

Just after giving birth, were you depressed or manic, or did you have hallucinations or a severe case of the "baby blues?"
What clinicians call postpartum depression or postpartum psychosis occurs more frequently in women with manic-depressive disorder than in women who have major depression alone.

When you're depressed, do you wake up depressed and feel better as the day goes on, or do you wake up okay and start feeling down later in the day?
In a depressive episode, bipolar patients feel worse as the day progresses. In contrast, depressed unipolar patients feel terrible in the morning; then, as the day goes on, the cloud lifts.

Have you ever noticed a seasonal course to your depressions? Do you get depressed in September, but not in April?
Some people who suffer from mood disorders find their depressions have seasonal patterns (sometimes called "winter blues" or more accurately *seasonal affective disorder*), especially if they live in an area with a long, dreary winter. You're at higher risk for a winter depression in Minnesota, for example, than in Florida.

Can you remember a time when a depression was preceded or followed by a sudden burst of energy, or even a few hours of feeling great?

This pattern suggests that your depression may be bipolar.

SCREEN YOUR FAMILY TREE

Because genes transmit manic-depressive disorder from parent to child, your family history is important. If one of your first-degree relatives (parents, siblings, or children) has manic-depressive symptoms, this fact has diagnostic significance, so be sure to tell your psychiatrist. We discuss genetic issues in Chapter Four.

Depression and mania can take various forms. Moreover, since family members often downplay or disguise their symptoms, looking for manic-depressive disorder in a family tree is not as simple as looking for diabetes.

Manic-depressive patients may find they have both depressed and manic-depressive relatives, or relatives diagnosed as psychotic, schizophrenic, or suffering from a schizoaffective disorder. In schizoaffective disorder, depressed or manic periods are complicated by delusions or hallucinations that don't fit the prevailing mood.

Relatives who abuse alcohol or drugs may have hidden mania or depression: People who suffer from mood swings often try to "medicate" themselves with alcohol, prescription pills, or street drugs.

Try to examine how your relatives relate to other people. Do any of them seem overly dependent on others? Do any have persistent, medically unexplained physical symptoms—stomachaches, headaches, or lower back pain? Sometimes dependent behavior or vague physical symptoms are clues to a hidden depressive disorder.

Mania can take the form of eccentricity, antisocial acts, conduct disorders in adolescents and children, delusions, and stormy interpersonal relationships (i.e., extramarital affairs, or juggling three jobs at the same time). You may know such a relative as the "black sheep" of the family.

To identify possible psychiatric disorders in relatives, you have to describe whatever *problems* run in the family. To a psychiatrist, even common terms like "nervous breakdown," "religious nut," "odd," "weird," "wild," or "overstressed" can convey important information.

STAN'S FAMILY: AN EXAMPLE

Stan had his first depression at age 14 and was hospitalized for three months. Over the next fourteen years he relapsed repeatedly and got little relief from medications. He was treated with electroshock three times. At age 28 he was referred to me, because I specialize in treatment-resistant patients.

Since Stan's first attack had occurred at such a young age, I suspected a manic-depressive disorder. I asked Stan about his family history. One of his uncles had been depressed, possibly a manic-depressive, but the family had lost touch with him.

His parents had divorced two years ago, and Stan described their marriage: wild laughing and singing, screaming spells, fist fights, and infidelity. I called Stan's father and had a chat with him; his description of his brother's spending sprees—buying two sailboats when he couldn't even meet his mortgage payments—indeed suggested manic-depressive disorder. I also learned that Stan's grandfather had committed suicide, jumping from a highway bridge right onto concrete. Stan's father was taking the antipsychotic medication thioridazine

(Mellaril) to calm himself down. But he warned me: "Don't tell Stan."

This family history, and Stan's symptoms, prompted me to add lithium to Stan's antidepressant medication regimen. The improvement was almost immediate. What had helped us was *diagnosing both Stan and his family*.

TEST YOUR CHILD

Parents frequently ignore the severity of mood swings in their child or adolescent. They assume moodiness is a part of growing up—and sometimes it is. Other times, though, it can point to a larger problem.

In 1921, Emil Kraepelin, a contemporary of Freud, recorded and described the symptoms and courses of various psychiatric illnesses. In the process, he studied the lives of 903 manic-depressive patients. He discovered that only 0.4 percent of these individuals had displayed manic-depressive symptoms before the age of 10, but 2.5 percent had clear symptoms between the ages of 10 and 15, and 16.4 percent had symptoms between the ages of 15 and 20. More recently, a study of manic-depressive adults showed that between 11 and 35 percent recalled having manic episodes in adolescence. Despite such findings, manic-depressive illness in children and teenagers continues to be diagnosed as conduct disorder, attention-deficit disorder, or oppositional defiant disorder.

THE CHILD BEFORE PUBERTY

1. Does your child seem overly shy or withdrawn, often not joining in the games of other children?

2. Does he go through restless periods when he's unable to sit still?
3. Does he take abnormal risks at play, such as jumping off high ledges?
4. Does he change his mind continually, liking something one day and hating it a week later?
5. Is he a discipline problem?
6. Does he get overly anxious or excited about coming events—i.e., school trips, visits to a friend's house?
7. Does he get into more fights than other children?
8. Does he cry a lot?

It is rare to find a young child who is depressed for six or seven weeks in a row; mood disturbances are less persistent in children than in adults. But moody children who will later be diagnosed as having a bipolar disorder display a great deal of emotional fluctuation. They like something today and hate it tomorrow. They're never sure how they feel. Also, when very young they may act hostile at the wrong times, and retreat at times when hostility may be appropriate.

Remember Kevin, the 7-year-old we met in Chapter One? When he was barely past the toddler stage, Kevin had problems empathizing with other children. If someone in nursery school fell down and hurt himself, for example, other children might run over to comfort him, but Kevin would be too absorbed in his own game to pay much attention. Kevin would often stand and cry helplessly when other boys fought with him. Then, when the children were playing nicely in a group, Kevin might grab a toy out of another boy's hands and, with no apparent provocation, hit him over the head with it.

With proper medication, however, Kevin felt better about himself. Medication didn't change him into a different child.

It merely gave him the ability to control himself and show his best side.

MANIC-DEPRESSIVE ADOLESCENTS

1. Is your teenager often irritable?
2. Does he seem to get angry too easily?
3. Does he seem more depressed or quiet than normal?
4. Do you find your kid often buying impulsively: five wristwatches at a time, clothes he'll never wear, records he'll never listen to?
5. Is he attempting to be "super-competent": running for class president when already editor of the school newspaper, president of the French club, concertmaster in the orchestra, and a part-time waiter at the diner?
6. Do you suspect that your teenager abuses drugs or alcohol?
7. Does he talk a lot about death or suicide, even jokingly?
8. Do his grades fluctuate widely from one report card to the next?
9. Have you noticed a sudden change in his activities?
10. Has he developed any interests that seem bizarre?

Both depressive and manic symptoms in adolescence are similar to those seen in adults. The one major difference, according to studies by doctors N.D. Ryan and J. Puig-Antich, is that manic adolescents more often have hallucinations or feelings of persecution.

OTHER SELF-TESTS

A psychiatrist may have you fill out a self-rating scale for depression that's somewhat similar to the self-tests we've seen in this chapter. The widely used Beck Depression Inventory, for example, lists twenty-one symptoms of depression for which you rate yourself on a scale of 0 (absent) to 3 (severe). Included are symptoms such as feelings of disappointment in yourself, sadness, crying, irritation, guilt, inability to make decisions, and dissatisfaction with your personal appearance. The Beck Inventory attempts to define how depressed you are.

TESTS PSYCHIATRISTS DO

To measure the severity of your depression a psychiatrist may use the Hamilton Depression Scale, which includes twenty-one items to be rated on a scale of 0 (absent) to 4 (extreme). Some ratings (for sleep pattern, anxiety, weight loss, or thoughts of suicide, for example) will depend on your answers to his questions. Others will reflect his impressions, such as how agitated you appear, or how much insight you seem to have into your condition. Depressed people usually score 15 or more on this scale; those who are severely depressed may score 25 or higher.

Mania in its less extreme forms can be harder to assess than depression. Clinicians frequently use two structured tests to measure the severity of mania.

The first, a Mania Rating Scale developed by R.C. Young, includes eleven items. It's similar to the Hamilton Depression Scale in that some ratings are based on what you tell the interviewer, while others are based on the interviewer's observations.

The second, a Manic Behavior Rating Scale, does not require your cooperation. Why? Because patients experiencing mania are sometimes uncooperative! You may not even be aware of it as the interviewer rates you for nine items (unrestrained behavior, hurried speech, elevated mood, feelings of superiority, dramatization, loudness, overexcitability, excess speech, and dominance) on a 9-degree scale of intensity.

The tests described in this chapter constitute only one aspect of the diagnostic process. Let's move on to discuss other diagnostic issues.

Chapter 3

HOW A PSYCHIATRIST VIEWS YOUR MOOD SWINGS

Psychiatrists and patients have different perspectives on manic-depressive disorder. The psychiatrist sees it as an illness, with characteristic signs and symptoms that cause suffering. The patient, particularly if he's newly diagnosed, sees his problem as a reaction to stress. Here is Martin's view of his manic-depressive disorder. . .

"In my early twenties, after I was hospitalized the first time, I could see how work—you know, the pressure, the rat race—made me more tired and irritable. I thought I knew all the answers. I said to myself, okay, work your way out of this one depression, then get a new job—you'll never have to go through this again. Some stress I can handle, but that job involved quite a bit of traveling. And I don't travel well. The kids were little, and I guess I missed being around them.

So I changed jobs. At first I was stressed out because

the job was new. Then when I finally got used to it, a new boss came in with a whole new set of demands, and I went into a miserable downer that lasted for months. Finally it seemed to work out.

It hit me like a ton of bricks again when I was in my early forties, and I landed back in the hospital. I don't know, at that point I must have been going through my midlife crisis—the children were almost grown, and I felt I couldn't handle aging. I worked my way through it that time, too.

From then on, the stress got to me every few years. I'm retiring soon, going to spend some time with my grandchildren. . . . I really should be enjoying this time of my life; I've worked hard to get here. But I can feel it, feel the stress creeping up again. I guess retirement really means my life is over."

WHAT THE PSYCHIATRIST SEES: FIRST THINGS FIRST

Martin is a 62-year-old accountant, married, the father of three grown children. When he comes for his first appointment I ask how I can help him. He tells me he is stressed out again, and gives me the account you've just read. I have to encourage him, because he talks slowly, a few words at a time. He complains of tiredness, and he shivers slightly even though the office is warm. He looks like a man in his eighties, not his sixties. Martin seems depressed, but I'm wondering about his physical health, too.

Since a psychiatrist is first a medical doctor, my first step is to check my patient, by examination and laboratory tests, for possible physical causes of psychiatric symptoms. In Martin's case, however, the physical exam and all lab tests are within normal limits. This includes thyroid disease, which had initially occurred to me as a possible cause of his present complaints.

When I find no medical illness, I evaluate all the patient's signs, symptoms, and behaviors, and figure out which specific psychiatric disorder is present.

DETERMINING THE PSYCHIATRIC DISORDER

Reading body language is part of the art of diagnostic assessment. Those unintentional facial expressions, postures, and gestures tell their own story. The manic patient may show so-called push of speech and flight of ideas: talking on and on, jumping from topic to topic, getting angry when interrupted. In contrast, a depressed patient may have a permanent frown—the "omega sign": a vertical forehead crease topped by a horizontal one—or a slumped, defeated look.

SYMPTOMS

A symptom is a complaint that causes you distress or interferes with normal functioning. Lack of concentration and a general loss of interest in life are symptoms of depression; overconfidence, racing thoughts, and feelings of elation are symptoms of mania. Psychiatrists classify all of these disturbances of mental well-being as *psychological* symptoms. They call disruptions in the body's physical functioning *vegetative* symptoms; examples are insomnia and loss of appetite.

BEHAVIOR

Let's assume a certain disturbance in your biochemical balance produces symptoms of depression. These symptoms set off a chain reaction that influences your behavior. For example, you may decide to skip work because you just don't have the energy. If the biochemical imbalance produces symptoms of mania, your behavior is quite different: you may start too many projects, spend money you don't really have, or suddenly change from a wallflower to a siren.

When Brenda, in Chapter Two, remembered the time she moved furniture around all night, she was exhibiting manic behavior. I would never have known about that incident, though, if she hadn't told me. Part of the psychiatrist's job is spending time with the patient, getting to know her, eliciting these kinds of memories.

THE NATURAL COURSE OF MANIC DEPRESSIVE DISORDER

We all are familiar with the natural course of the flu: a few days of fever, chills, and maybe diarrhea, then a few more days of weakness and fatigue as the body recovers. The natural course of manic-depressive disorder is more difficult to predict. Even the onset is quite variable—either mania or depression may cause the first hospitalization. However, a few basic features seem standard.

• Patients with bipolar II disorder (major depression alternating with hypomania) tend to have more severe depressive episodes than other manic-depressive patients. However, their illness is *not* likely to transform into bipolar I disorder (major depression alternating with severe mania).

Fewer than 5 percent of bipolar II patients will ever experience incapacitating mania.

DOUBLE TROUBLE: PERSONALITY DISORDERS

Incapacitated, depressed people rely heavily on family and friends. A woman suffering from depression may want to stay in bed all day. But if her husband coaxes her up and encourages her to make him breakfast, pack a lunch, and join friends later for a movie, she may drag along. This pattern may continue for months before the depression becomes so incapacitating that she can no longer comply with her husband's wishes. At this point he may bring her to a therapist.

Even if her depression is due to an inherited predisposition, her exaggerated reliance on her husband during the depression may have reinforced an underlying "dependent personality disorder." Just as dependency can develop as part of a chronic physical illness, it may also appear as a complication of a long-lasting mood disorder. While the depression may respond to medication, the dependent personality disorder requires psychological counseling.

The revised third edition of the *Diagnostic and Statistical Manual of Mental Disorders* (DSM-III-R), the standard handbook of psychiatric diagnosis, lists a dozen different personality disorders. A psychiatrist's complete diagnosis of a patient may include both a major psychiatric disorder (i.e., major depression or manic-depressive illness) and a personality disorder, if applicable.

- Bipolar I and bipolar II disorder are both *recurrent* illnesses. Most patients with manic-depressive disorder will experience between ten and fifteen incapacitating episodes of depression or mania over the course of a lifetime. There's no predicting how long episodes will last—anywhere from a week to more than two years.
- Unlike patients with schizophrenia, most people with manic-depressive disorder have sustained periods of normalcy between episodes. During these normal periods they may function very well indeed—often better than people who periodically suffer from depression only—but never mania. A person with a bipolar disorder, perhaps driven by the energy of hypomania, may be a successful politician, artist, or businessman.
- Although some patients experience either depression or mania as frequently as the season changes, others go for many years between episodes. The highest risk of relapse seems to be shortly after recovery—about 25 percent of manic-depressive patients have a relapse within three months. As times goes on, the risk of relapse recedes.
- "Late-onset bipolar disorder" can strike people in their sixties and seventies, but most cases of manic-depressive illness are diagnosed in young adults in their twenties. As diagnostic procedures get refined, more children and adolescents will be found to have bipolar disorder.
- Recurrences appear to be more closely spaced in older people than in the young. A problem with establishing figures for recurrence is that episodes may be quite dissimilar. It's possible for a patient to overlook a hypomanic episode entirely, especially if he is preoccupied during this time with heavy drinking or the sudden appearance of a phobia.

THE COURSE OF MARTIN'S DISORDER

Let's go back to Martin, the depressed 62-year-old accountant. Interestingly, he told me that during his very first episode of depression he tended to overeat and oversleep. Was Martin's a bipolar illness?

Initially I didn't think so. Martin had been married to the same woman for more than forty years, had switched jobs only three times in his lifetime, and was well liked at work. He had none of the stormy interpersonal relations that characterize so many manic-depressive people. Yet his poor response to previous treatment with antidepressant medication suggested that his was not a typical unipolar depression.

To refine my diagnosis I gave Martin a series of chemical tests (more about these in Chapter Six). The results, in his case, were inconclusive, but I still wasn't ready to give up.

FAMILY TIES

Discussion during our second meeting revealed that Martin's paternal grandfather had been a problem drinker with a violent temper, who on at least two occasions had foolishly misspent prodigious sums of family money. His wife, Martin's grandmother, was a volatile, twice-divorced dancer. These anecdotes strengthened my suspicions that Martin had an inherited susceptibility to a manic-depressive disorder.

DIGGING FOR CLUES

Over the next three weeks Martin and his wife came to see me four times. At each visit, I asked if they could recall a time when Martin had acted completely out of character. It was important to ask his wife, too. Often, when a patient describes such a period, it sounds as though he had simply experienced a great time. But a close relative may have an entirely different perspective on the incident.

I asked more specific questions. Had Martin ever lost a lot of money at the racetrack? No. Had he ever received several speeding tickets in a row? No. Had he ever had a period of unusual sexual activity? No.

Well, yes, maybe one time. Years ago, at the age of 28, Martin had stopped at a bar for a drink on his lunch hour. He met a prostitute there, and they took off together. At that time Martin had just emerged from his first depression. "It felt like I'd been through hell," he said, "and now I needed to be horizontal for a few days before I could stand up straight again." After a week of hectic traveling with stops in Reno and Las Vegas, Martin went home, sheepishly confessed everything to his wife . . . and that was that. Nothing of the sort ever happened again.

Very interesting. Hypersexuality is a common expression of mania. In light of Martin's family history and his persistent depression, this one sexual escapade—close on the heels of a depression—suggested a bipolar II disorder. I began to treat Martin's illness as such. *Two months later, all his symptoms of depression had completely vanished.*

As we're beginning to see, manic-depressive illness can take many forms. Teasing out the diagnostic clues can be an intricate task. Let's do a thumbnail sketch of four different variations.

VARIATION #1: MANIA PLUS AGGRESSION

Ten-year-old Larry tells his mother he's so happy he feels he could fly. What's more, he climbs up on a cabinet intending to show her. She restrains him. Immediately he begins screaming and punching at her, and at others who try to intervene.

Upset and exasperated, his mother phones me to describe the incident. "Doctor," she says, "You are wrong about Larry having manic-depressive disorder. He's just a hostile brat."

"Well," I replied. "When manic, Larry is joyful, exuberant, full of ideas. But if someone tries to interfere with his goals, he can instantly get angry and aggressive. This is apparently what happened."

Peter, a businessman, is in an expansive mood but doesn't realize he's manic. He stops in at his favorite clothes shop and buys three expensive suits that he can't afford. As he starts to leave, he realizes his wife will criticize this spending spree. In sudden despair and exasperation, he opens the box and begins ripping and tearing at the suits. The manager tries to reason with him. Peter grabs and tears the manager's jacket. By the time the police arrive Peter is tearing suits off the racks, wrecking anything he can get his hands on.

Peter's wife, distraught, comes to me for a consultation. "Is his true character coming to light?" she asks me. "Or is he on drugs?"

"No," I tell her, "this is manic behavior. When a patient who's manic feels restrained, he may explode just as Peter did. If Peter complies with his treatment, though, there's a good chance this will never happen again."

VARIATION #2:   MANIC-DEPRESSIVE DISORDER PLUS PSYCHOSIS

"They're trying to kill me," Gail sobs to her daughter. "They're forcing me to kill myself. They almost got me, they almost made me drive off the road a few hours ago, but I turned the wheel back just in the nick of time. I'm petrified. Usually they let up after a day or two, but they didn't this time. They're going to get me, I know they are. Somebody help me, please!"

Her daughter, horrified, asks who "they" are.

"I've never met them," Gail says, "and I can't see them. They're these loud voices in my head, male voices. But not any men I know. They're low-lifes, like the guys you see hanging outside bars, taunting women. Only it's me they're after, just me. First they wanted me to have sex with them, all at once, but I refused. Now they keep saying they're going to kill me. They say things like, 'See that window, you're going to jump, you want to jump, don't you?' and then they laugh, belly laughs. I can't stand it anymore."

Gail's daughter calls me, frantic. "My mother was diagnosed as having manic-depressive disorder four years ago, but these 'voices' are new. Is she turning schizophrenic? Will she ever be all right again?"

Yet Gail insisted the voices pursued her not when she was depressed, but when she felt high. Three months after her mood had stabilized, she was still hearing voices. We rediagnosed her condition as a schizoaffective disorder, and treated her accordingly.

"She's not listening to me," Stuart raged. His wife had brought him to the hospital, and he stood in the emergency room screaming, "Make her respond to me. Don't let her do this to me." According to his wife, Stuart was the only one who was 'doing' anything—he'd begun picking up random objects and throwing them at her.

First I diagnosed a schizoaffective disorder in Stuart, too. But I eventually discovered that his thoughts were so "loud," he assumed his wife could hear them. When she did not answer them, he felt ignored. That's when he began throwing things around in frustration.

Stuart's reaction, while extreme, was nonetheless typical of a person experiencing a *psychotic manic episode*. Someone in this state might have delusions of grandeur—for example, believing himself to be Napoleon with a special mission to accomplish.

A person in a *psychotic depressed episode*, on the other hand, might delude himself that he had killed his mother, and therefore deserved to pay with his own life.

In the hospital, after calming down, Stuart was embarrassed about his unreasonable behavior. He made comments such as "I'm losing my mind," "I'm going off the deep end," and "I'm afraid I'm really crazy." His insight into his condition further supported that he was suffering from manic-depressive disorder, not schizophrenia or a schizoaffective disorder. After four weeks of treatment in the hospital, he went back to work and functioned normally.

VARIATION #3: MANIC-DEPRESSIVE DISORDER OR ATTENTION-DEFICIT HYPERACTIVITY DISORDER?

Neil is 8 years old and hyperactive. At age 5, he was suspended from kindergarten for throwing a chair at the teacher. At age 7, he was diagnosed as having *attention-deficit hyperactivity disorder*. His parents report that he can be happy one moment, then go into a tantrum over nothing a moment later. He cries a lot. His teachers say he seldom pays attention in class, turns in sloppy papers, and forgets to do homework. One doctor had prescribed Ritalin, a stimulant that often helps kids with attention-deficit hyperactivity disorder. The medication did help Neil to pay a little more attention in class, but it did nothing to change his tendency toward temper tantrums and crying spells.

Most child psychiatrists agree that attention-deficit hyperactivity disorder is a hodgepodge diagnosis. One condition sometimes associated with it is *minimal brain damage (MBD)*. We observed Neil and watched his movements closely. We asked him to draw a picture and saw him set to work. Now, if he'd had MBD, his tongue would probably have emerged from his mouth and followed his hand as he drew, but nothing of the sort happened. We asked him to make specific movements with his left hand, and he made them without trouble, while his right hand remained inactive. If he'd had MBD, there would have been an "overflow," the right hand mirroring the movements of the left. So we could rule out MBD in Neil's case.

Neil's hyperactivity seemed to be psychiatric, not neurological. It looked like the same hyperactivity found in adult patients with bipolar disorder. If we were to see Neil again in twenty years, his hyperactivity would probably still be there, but by that time his suffering would have a new name: *manic-depressive disorder.*

In addition, we came across an interesting diagnostic clue: Neil's mother was manic-depressive.

In treating Neil, we worked on the assumption that he had manic-depressive disorder or a precursor to it. We continued Ritalin to help him pay attention in school, and we added lithium to control his moods and outbursts of temper. The improvement was striking.

VARIATION #4:   MANIC-DEPRESSIVE DISORDER OR CONDUCT DISORDER?

Sixteen-year-old Jessica recently had her second abortion. Twice before, she had been suspended from school because of promiscuous behavior. Yet at other times teachers reported that she was a model student. Her parents tell us, "Weeks will go by where Jess is a pleasure to be with. Then she'll get upset over some little thing, like being asked to hang up her jacket. She'll steal money from my wallet, storm out of the house, and come back three or four days later. When we ask where she was, she'll scream that it's none of our business, that she's old enough to choose her own friends and stay with them. Then sometimes she'll mope around the house for two or three weekends in a row. When we suggest calling a friend, she says no one likes her and she has no friends."

We diagnosed Jessica's *conduct disorder* as the equivalent of a manic-depressive disorder, and treated her with lithium. She began concentrating more on schoolwork. She lost her compulsion to have sex with every boy who asked her out. All's well that ends well, you might say. What we questioned was the diagnosis of conduct disorder.

Some therapists diagnose manic-depressive disorder in an adolescent only when there are clear periods of mania, including elation and grandiose ideas. However, anger and irritability are two other ways in which mania often shows up in both teenagers and adults. These are precisely the states we may erroneously blame on environmental stresses.

In their book on childhood and adolescent psychiatry, *When Acting Out Isn't Acting*, Drs. Lynne W. Weisberg and Rosalie Greenberg recommend lithium in "treating antisocial children, since it helps reduce aggression. Lithium has been shown to help in cases of conduct-disordered children who are given to aggressive and explosive outbursts. Children whose parents respond well to lithium appear to respond especially well to lithium treatment."

TEENAGE DEPRESSION

A diagnosis of unipolar depression in a teenager should lead us to search for evidence of a possible bipolar disorder. We know that depression is often associated with mania. Many manic-depressive patients have their first depression in adolescence. A follow-up study on 60 adolescents (13 to 16 years old) hospitalized for depression showed that four years later, 20 percent had been rediagnosed as manic-depressive. Professionals are increasingly aware that if a person suffers from depression at age 15, there's a high probability that later in life he will experience manic symptoms as well. The patient should be on the lookout for those symptoms, and should come for treatment when they emerge.

Diagnosis of mania in a child or a teenager points to a need for long-term follow-up. A doctor should observe the relationship of depressed periods to the normal or excited periods, how long each cycle lasts, and how severely the youngster is affected. If it's started early enough, proper treatment can probably prevent him from quitting school—or committing suicide. If treated, a young person is less likely to experience later marital difficulties and job problems.

A PSYCHIATRIST'S PERSPECTIVE
ON MOODINESS

"My friends criticize me because I'm moody," says Lynn. "They think I'm the kind of person that just 'lets it all hang out.' They don't realize I'm really trying to control myself. Can a psychiatrist help?"

Yes, he can. Psychiatrists call Lynn's condition cyclothymia (bipolar III disorder). The periods of mania and depression rarely last more than a week, and there are normal periods in between. Moods set in unexpectedly— "just like the weather," as one of Dr. Hagop S. Akiskal's patients described it. Many cyclothymic people experience about equal amounts of hypomania and depression; a fair number, however, have more depression.

Dr. Frederick K. Goodwin reported that cyclothymic patients in one study experienced a "phase advance" as they switched from depression into hypomania: "Coincident with and following the switch," he wrote, "they were getting up earlier and going to bed earlier each day." Patients suffering from these less severe, but continual mood swings are at risk for alcohol and drug abuse.

COMPARE YOUR VIEWPOINT WITH THE
PYSCHIATRIST'S

This chapter has emphasized the contrast between the average person's perceptions of manic-depressive disorder and the psychiatrist's professional perspective.

In the Middle Ages, patients with seizure disorder, schizophrenia, and some forms of bipolar disorder were thought to be possessed. Some were even burned at the stake! Today's "enlightened" attitude rejects notions of witchcraft and possession, but there's still a good deal of misunderstanding. Psychiatric patients are often considered weak or inferior. Patients may feel forced to hide their psychiatric disorder; families are embarrassed; insurance companies try to withhold coverage. Candidates for public office who have received psychiatric care know disclosure of that information could deal their campaign a devastating blow. Parents and teachers are quick to use labels such as "lazy" and "performing below potential" (for a depressed child), "oppositional," "defiant," or "hyperactive" (for a manic youngster), or "out of it," "crazy," or "drug abuser" (for a person who has delusions or hallucinations).

Education is still desperately needed to raise public awareness of psychiatric conditions and arouse compassion for patients. More knowledge could save careers, and even lives.

What can **you** do? Before rejecting or punishing a troubled person, talk to an expert. Get the psychiatrist's view of what's going on.

Chapter 4

Broken Homes and Broken Genes

INSIDE THE ROLLER COASTER:
8-YEAR-OLD KEVIN

"**W**hy? Why? Why? I cry for no reason. I'm angry for no reason. I feel so bad. Two days ago I was so excited, I felt so good. Dad kept saying, 'Shut up, Kevin, shut up.'

Now I'm down again. I feel like I did something bad. I don't know what. He cries.

I wish Mom would yell at me, do something, anything. She's been in her bedroom for three weeks, hardly ever leaving. Daddy blames me, says it's my fault, says it happened right after I was born. That's when she didn't wanna come out of her room and she ended up in the hospital. Maybe now she'll go to the hospital again. Daddy told Aunt Sally what the doctor said: 'Mom had the baby blues.'

Mom and me are just the same. We feel sad for no reason. I'm not like other kids. I can't go outside and play like my sisters. I hate 'em, hate 'em, hate 'em. Take that, and that, and that." (Makes a fist and pounds his head.)

I have known Kevin for nearly a year now. What strikes me about him? He can answer my questions about his moods. He knows they change without reason, and he knows he can't do anything about it—no matter how much he hates it, no matter how much he wants to change. He had been hospitalized before, and a child psychiatrist had diagnosed him as manic-depressive.

LIKE MOTHER, LIKE SON?

Kevin's mother suffers from manic-depressive disorder, too. Her two older children don't show any symptoms, but Kevin has enough for all of them put together. Why just Kevin? If, as some people assume, depression is a result of environment—if it's learned from the parents, for instance—then why should only one child in a family be affected, and not the other children also?

Is it because Kevin's mother was more depressed during his upbringing? No. One of the sisters is older than Kevin by only a year. Is it because Kevin is closer to his mother than his sisters are? That's hard to measure, but it doesn't seem likely. When his mother is depressed she's very distant—she wants to stay away from all three kids.

Is there a better explanation for Kevin's mood swings? Yes, we think so. Kevin hasn't copied or learned his mother's mood swings; he has actually *inherited her disposition*. Before we look at the evidence, let's examine another patient, Mary.

BROKEN HOMES AS THE ONLY CAUSE?

Mary, a teenager, was taken to the hospital after a suicide attempt. Friends, neighbors, teachers all say the same thing: "Look at the family, what can you expect? She comes from a broken home. Her father is an alcoholic; her mother has different lovers in the house every night. No wonder the kid has problems!"

Science disagrees. Mary lives in a broken home, all right, but more importantly, she carries the same genetic structure as her parents. Adoption studies support the view that Mary's father did not become an alcoholic because there were problems at home, but primarily because his inherited body chemistry primed him for alcohol abuse. Mary's mother is not promiscuous because her marriage failed; she is by nature emotionally unstable and unable to settle down in a marriage. Obviously, the broken home hasn't helped Mary deal with her problems. But it's not the sole cause of those problems, either.

Look at the families that lived through World War II. In Europe as well as in the United States, most fathers left for combat and many were killed. Proportionally, there were more broken up homes during that period than there are now. But the mothers went to work, and the children learned to provide for themselves. An economic recovery followed the war, and these same children became hard-working, capable people. They didn't have an unusually high incidence of psychiatric disorders. If broken homes were the cause of psychiatric illness, surely that wartime generation could not have coped with adversity so well.

Recent studies of manic-depressive disorder have tried to separate the influences of environment from those of genetic makeup. As we'll see, the results clearly point to a strong genetic link.

FIRST: FAMILY STUDIES

Family studies measure the incidence of psychiatric disorders in the blood relatives of psychiatric patients—that is, in people from the same gene pool. Since only about 0.5 percent of the general population (1 out of every 200 people) will ever develop a manic-depressive disorder, and the overall risk for affective illness (either depressive or manic-depressive disorder) is 2 to 3 percent, any rate above these levels suggests a familial tie—which might be either genetically transmitted or learned through living in the same family.

A review of seven studies found an overall *15 percent* incidence of affective illness in the relatives of bipolar patients. These studies support, but do not prove, the inheritability of bipolar disorders.

Investigators have studied the more distant blood relatives of mood-disordered patients, looking for risk factors, probabilities, and different disguises a disorder might assume; a father's alcoholism, for instance, may surface as a particular type of depression in one of his daughters.

When a mood disorder is diagnosed in one family member, the risk that parents, siblings, or children will develop symptoms increases two- or threefold over the 0.5 percent risk to the general population—but that's still a fairly low figure. If one parent and one child are diagnosed, however, there is a 25 percent chance that any other child will develop symptoms as well.

What does all this mean for you? If you have a first-degree relative (parent, sibling, or child) with manic-depressive disorder, there is a 7 to 10 percent chance you may develop the same disorder, and an 8 to 10 percent chance you may develop depression.

Investigators have also examined the effect on the children

when a parent has a manic-depressive disorder. In one study of seven boys, each with one manic-depressive parent, it was found that by age 2½, these boys hit and hurt their friends more often than children with normal parents. Furthermore, they showed an unusual pattern of emotional reactions. At times when anger was appropriate, they often failed to react. They got unusually upset when adults got into an argument, but showed no relief when the argument was resolved. Children with normal parents had just the opposite reactions.

Even though both depression and manic-depressive disorder cluster in families, how do we know there is a genetic link? Critics point out that if parents speak Russian, there is a high likelihood their children will, too. Learning rather than genetics may be the important factor. To deal with this question, let's take a look at the results of twin studies.

SECOND: TWIN STUDIES

There are two kinds of twins. *Identical* twins share the same genes. *Fraternal* twins do not; they are genetically no more alike than regular brothers or sisters. The frequency with which both twins share a given trait is called the *concordance rate*. If a mood disorder is mainly genetic, identical twins should show a higher concordance rate for it than fraternal twins. But if the mood disorder is mainly a learned behavior, the concordance rates should be about the same in identical and fraternal twins.

In comparative studies of manic-depressive disorder in identical and fraternal twins, higher concordance rates were found in identical twins, suggesting that a genetic link does in fact exist.

In 1989, Drs. Donald W. Goodwin and Samuel B. Guze

tallied the results of nine mood-disorders-in-twins studies, the first of which had been conducted in 1928. Their report covered 83 manic-depressive patients who had identical twins; 72 percent of the identical twins were found to be manic-depressive as well. By contrast, out of 226 manic-depressive fraternal twins, only 14 percent had a twin who was also manic-depressive.

"Wait a moment," the skeptic protests. "How can you be sure that *shared genes* account for these higher concordance rates in identical twins? After all, twins who look alike get treated alike and live with roughly equal levels of stress. Maybe that's why both of them tend to suffer from the same mood disorder."

To explore this question, investigators looked for twins who had not grown up together.

Dr. Ross Baldessarini studied twelve pairs of identical twins who were *separated at birth and reared apart*. In nine of these cases (75 percent), when he detected manic-depressive illness in one twin, he subsequently discovered it in the other twin. This finding strengthened the argument that the origin of manic-depressive disorder is genetic, not environmental.

Twin-study results also suggest that manic-depressive illness is clinically quite distinct from "unipolar" major depression. If one twin developed manic-depressive illness, the other twin was likely to develop it, too—*not* major depression alone. Similarly, if one twin suffered from major depression, that's what the other twin was likely to develop—*not* manic-depressive illness.

Judging by concordance rates, manic-depressive illness is more easily inheritable than unipolar depression. Seventy-five percent of identical and 14 percent of fraternal twins are concordant for bipolar (manic-depressive) disorder, while only 40 percent of identical and 11 percent of fraternal twins are concordant for unipolar (major depressive) disorder.

WHAT'S THE MORAL OF ALL THESE STUDIES?

No matter what your approach, the results of these three types of studies suggest that genetic factors are at least partly responsible for a predisposition to mood disorders. A recent twin study adds punch to the genetic theory.

Psychologists at the University of Minnesota compared identical and fraternal twins reared together and reared apart. Before the study, some of the subjects hadn't even known they had a twin. The investigators made a striking discovery: *Identical twins reared apart were more similar in many of their preferences, tastes, abilities, skills, and behaviors than identical twins who grew up together.*

What can this mean? Here's one possible interpretation: When you see your identical twin, your "mirror image," every day, you may fight that image as a way of clarifying your own identity. But when your "mirror image" is unknown to you and lives many miles away, there's no reason to protest. Genes in their unadulterated power prevail.

The strong genetic underpinning of mood disorders and other psychiatric disorders has led us to explore the genetics of body chemistry. Today, psychiatrists can often correct mood disorders that are caused by chemical processes gone astray. We discuss psychopharmacology—(the use of mood-changing medications)—in Chapter Seven.

GENETICS: THE DIRECT LINKS

Our genes, carried on microscopic bodies called chromo-somes, are organic messengers that carry our inherited features—sex, height, eye color, hair color, and many, many others. For each trait, a person inherits two genes—one from the mother and one from the father. One gene is stronger, or "dominant;" the other is weaker, or "recessive." It's the information on the dominant gene that shows up; we say it is *expressed*. The recessive gene's information is suppressed.

According to studies of the extended families of manic-depressive people, the gene for manic-depressive illness appears to be dominant. However, not every person who carries the gene for bipolar disorder will actually get sick with bipolar disorder. For instance, in the Amish study that we discuss in detail later, only 85 percent of suspected carriers in one extensively studied family became ill. Geneti-cists call the percentage of people who get sick—out of all those who carry the gene for the disorder—the *penetrance* of the gene. Penetrance can vary from 100 percent down to 50 percent. In the Amish study, the penetrance for the bipolar gene was estimated to be 60 to 70 percent.

The reasons for incomplete penetrance are not fully known. Certain other genes may encourage or inhibit the appearance of the disorder.

Genes are responsible for directing the building of our body and brain, and for the functioning of our brain chemis-try. In turn, the brain chemistry influences our moods, determining—among other things—whether we will suffer from depressive or manic-depressive disorder.

Since genes are merely tiny segments of chromosomes, it's much easier to locate the chromosome involved in a disorder than to pinpoint the specific gene thought to cause the disorder. Janice A. Egeland's landmark study of manic-depressive illness among the Amish population suggests that chromosome 11 is involved in that particular strain of the disorder. It's still uncertain whether her findings are only true for this homogeneous group of people, or whether they tell us something about manic-depressive disorder in general.

Currently, scientists are discussing whether manic-depressive illness is carried on a single gene, or on several genes whose pattern determines the expression of the disorder. Theoretically, less severe forms of the illness—such as cyclothymic or bipolar II disorder—might involve only some of the genes that together cause bipolar I disorder. However, both Egeland's study and our own research suggest that bipolar I and bipolar II disorder are actually caused by different genes.

As we will see in Chapter Six, various medications can correct the chemical imbalances of manic-depressive disorder. The closer we get to pinpointing the precise gene at work, and identifying the faulty proteins it produces, the closer we move toward discovering even more effective medications.

For instance, chromosome 11 seems to contain the gene for an enzyme called tyrosine hydroxylase. This enzyme helps to transform the amino acid tyrosine (necessary for life, and available only from the foods we eat) into dopamine and norepinephrine, two neurotransmitters that carry messages through nerve pathways in the brain. Medications that cause norepinephrine to accumulate in the spaces between brain cells—the synaptic clefts—are effective in treating depression, whether unipolar or bipolar. Therefore, scientists suspect that the gene for manic-depressive disorder and for the enzyme tyrosine hydroxylase sit close together, or are even one and the same. In other words, people with manic-depressive disorders may have a form of this enzyme that over- or underproduces dopamine and norepinephrine. During times of underproduction, a person with the defective enzyme feels depressed; during overproduction, he feels manic.

Why did we call this chapter "Broken Homes and Broken Genes"? Because we now understand why manic-depressive disorder is so often found in broken homes. We understand why the mother or father of a manic-depressive patient so typically leads a miserable life, has a marriage filled with turmoil, and eventually seeks divorce. The compelling reason is that broken genes—the genes associated with manic-depressive disorder—are responsible for *both* the child's illness and the family's tumultuous lifestyle.

BEYOND GENETICS

You may recall from our previous discussion that in identical twins who have identical genes, manic-depressive disorder in one twin also occurs in the other twin in 72 percent of all cases. If we suspect that a dominant gene with a penetrance of 72 percent is responsible for manic-depressive disorder, then the results of the twin studies corroborate those of extended-family studies.

But what about the other 28 percent of all cases? If these twins of manic-depressive patients do have the genetic vulnerability or predisposition, as we assume they must, then why don't they have the illness itself?

Think of a person sitting on a roller coaster, waiting for it to start. All the wiring is complete, the genetic arrangement for roller coaster moods is ready to go into action, but nothing moves until the attendant pushes the proper button. We suspect that in some people who have all the genes for manic-depressive illness, certain other genes play a *protective* role—keeping the attendant from pushing the button, so to speak. We also suspect that various harmful environmental influences can *knock out* the influences of these protective genes, rendering them useless and allowing the roller coaster attendant to push the "Go" button.

This is where the problems of everyday living may come into play. But what are the environmental factors that might trigger a manic-depressive disorder? What does it take to knock those "protector" genes?

Chapter 5

Stress and Mood Disorders

"**D**on has done nothing but lie around the house since he was fired from his job two months ago," his wife says. "He won't go apply for another job, won't help with the kids, won't fix up the house. If something doesn't change soon, I'll be seriously considering divorce." She can't understand why Don is like this—especially since he's been complaining for the past two years that he hates his job and wants a better one.

Iris, a secretary, is on cloud nine: she has won $15,000 in the lottery—a whole year's earnings! She dances and sings in the office, bubbles with energy throughout the day, and seems to need no sleep at night. It's easy to understand Iris' ecstatic high. All her friends and neighbors congratulate her and marvel at her luck.

Lynn and her best friend, Janet, have worked for the same company for ten years. They've always covered for each other when one takes time off or goes on vacation. This time, when

Janet returns to work after taking two weeks off, she finds her friend a nervous wreck. Lynn makes a few terse, bitter remarks about the extra work she had to do, but refuses to have a heart-to-heart talk. Janet is baffled.

Rhonda hasn't been herself for the past month. She thinks she's coming down with the flu, but it doesn't happen. On Thursday she wakes up and finds she doesn't even have the energy to get out of bed. It finally hits her as she glances at the calender—today is March 10th. So that's what's wrong—this is the anniversary of her father's death. She thought she had worked through her grief over her father's death years ago, but she obviously hasn't. Otherwise it wouldn't be dragging her down like this.

SHIFTING THE BLAME

Don, Iris, Lynn, and Rhonda all have one thing in common: They attribute their highs and lows to stress or to unusual events in their lives. We live in a society that probes for the reasons behind feelings. Therefore we invent and accept all kinds of make do explanations for abnormal moods—conscious or unconscious.

People who search their past and present life for reasons why they suffer from depression—or mania, for that matter—may really be suffering from a biochemical imbalance. It's possible that medications could control the imbalance that's the origin of their suffering.

STRESS RESULTING FROM DEPRESSION

Let's analyze Don's condition. He and his wife both thought he sank into a deep depression because he was let go from his job. Of course, feeling down is a typical reaction to losing a job. But usually the person recovers in a few days and then moves on to seek new work. This depression, which has continued for two months and has dragged Don so far down that he doesn't want to leave the house, is *not* a normal reaction to being fired.

Was it really the job loss that triggered a major depression in Don? Let's question his wife. She remembers that he had complained about his job for the past two years, had been irritable, had lost weight, and wasn't sleeping well. This leads us to suspect that Don's depression began long before he was fired.

After getting Don's written consent, we call his former boss. The boss tells us that Don's long history of low energy, negative attitude, irritability, and incapacitating headaches had been a drain on the company. Several months ago, Don fell behind again in ordering warehouse supplies, and this proved to be the last straw. He was fired.

We assume that at this point Don no longer tried to hold himself together, and his depression became incapacitating. Thus, the loss of his job was not the stressful trigger for the depression, but the result or consequence of a long-standing depression.

"LUCK" RESULTING FROM MANIA

Mildly manic symptoms can be misinterpreted in much the same way. Remember Iris, the lottery winner? Not even Iris herself realized that she had been feeling high for several weeks before her big win. So high, in fact, that she had gone out and blown her vacation money on a thousand lottery tickets—a reckless act that was quite uncharacteristic of her. Fortunately, the goddess of luck smiled on Iris. After winning $15,000, she had a perfect reason for feeling wonderful.

Iris' unusual burst of energy didn't stop here, though. She was feeling so good that the next week, $15,000 in hand, she went out and tried to make a down payment on a $300,000 house. Iris was lucky again. The bank loan officers realized that she had almost no savings and very few assets. Figuring that her secretarial job would never cover the expenses of this house, they refused to give her the mortgage. Other people are not so lucky. In periods like this, they take on greater financial obligations than they can handle—and then have to live with the consequences.

Iris' behavior shows three clear signs of hypomania: (1) her social judgment is poor; (2) while there might be cause for celebration, her excitement is out of proportion; and (3) like many other uncontrollably excited people, she does not want to take no for an answer. By the time she leaves the bank she is threatening to sue for discrimination against women.

STRESS AS A MAGNIFIER OF DEPRESSION

"My friend Janet wonders why I feel so horrible," Lynn says. "She keeps saying that we've each taken vacations dozens of times during the past ten years, and there's never been a problem. That just shows how insensitive she really is. She can't understand how disgusted I felt—disgusted with *myself*—when I found I collapsed under the extra work load. For two weeks straight I went home from work, crawled into bed, just to toss and turn without sleep. If Janet was feeling that horrible about herself, she'd avoid other people, too. But she just can't grasp what a failure I am."

What neither of them understands is that Lynn had been feeling depressed for weeks before Janet went out on vacation.

It's because Lynn was already depressed and listless that she could not handle the extra work, or ask for help. The increased workload didn't cause Lynn's depression. It merely *magnified* her depression, bringing it forcefully to her attention.

STRESS AS A TIME MARKER

What about Rhonda? Did she have an "anniversary depression"? Indeed, there is such a term in the psychiatric literature.

We asked Rhonda about previous years.

"Well, I loved my father a lot," she answered. "When the first anniversary of his death came around, I delayed my vacation for a day to go to the cemetery and take him roses, which he always loved. And I cried on his grave. But later, on my vacation, I went scuba diving in Hawaii and had a great time. Over the last few years I even forgot the day, and went to the cemetery as much as a month later. My kids were home from college—there was just too much going on."

"What about this year?"

"Well, this year it was different. It started in February. I felt weak, had no energy, and was just dragging along. I wasn't even looking forward to having the kids home on spring break. I couldn't understand it. I never had a depression in February or March. My two previous ones came in the fall, six years apart."

"But you think the anniversary of your father's death caused it?"

"Well, I was thinking about his death all the time—and I remembered that a counselor once told me there is such a thing as anniversary depression. It never affected me, though, until this year—if that's what this is. Do you think that's the explanation?"

"Frankly, no," I said. "I believe, Rhonda, that in your need to find a reason for your depression you latched onto an event that coincided with it. My patients do that all the time."

STRESS AS A SCAPEGOAT

The stories of Don, Iris, Lynn, and Rhonda show us that in a person with mood disorder, a particular life event can be mistaken for the cause of a mood shift.

Don didn't get depressed because he was fired; he lost his job because of poor performance due to depression.

Iris wasn't filled with unusual energy and excitement because of her luck in the lottery; her ecstasy predated the lottery win.

Lynn didn't fall apart because of extra work when her friend went on vacation; the increased workload just magnified her preexisting depression, causing temporary dysfunction.

And Rhonda? She put one and one together and got three: "anniversary depression" as the plausible explanation for her continuing low mood.

STRESS AS A TRIGGER OF DEPRESSION

"To tell you the truth, I expected Harriet might need to see a psychiatrist before she got through the first year of college," the teenage girl's mother said. "She has always been different from her sisters, always particular, always a perfectionist. She has a hard time adjusting. For instance, when our family moved to Kansas, Harriet was thirteen years old and her sisters were fifteen and ten. The other two enjoyed the move, got excited about having their own rooms, and made new friends easily. Harriet moped around all summer, and when school started she had to be pushed to go. It was almost Christmas before she brought her first friend home."

A patient like Harriet is sometimes said to suffer from an *adjustment disorder with depressed mood*—a condition in which symptoms are too few or too mild to constitute major depression. Harriet acted depressed and withdrawn, but her appetite and sleep patterns were undisturbed, she had no feelings of guilt or thoughts of suicide, and her level of self-esteem was acceptable.

But wait! An adjustment disorder normally develops suddenly in reaction to a significant life change. Yet Harriet's mother predicted that her daughter would need help. She saw something in Harriet that she didn't see in her other two daughters. What was it?

PERSONALITY DISORDER AND STRESS

Harriet's mother hit on a crucial point: Harriet *is* different. She is set in her ways and unable to handle new situations easily. Depression was her response to the move to Kansas—and to her freshman year at college. Harriet's personality made her vulnerable to change. As we found out, her father, an accountant, was the same way. She had inherited his rigidity. Harriet was depressed all summer. She didn't really believe she could adjust to college, but she couldn't say that to her parents. It had been the same when she was thirteen: she was so upset about the prospect of moving that she no longer wanted to see her friends. She withdrew from people months before the actual move.

Major life events are often the first things people point to as causes or triggers of their depression. Researchers exploring mood disorders among students have reported that one out of every five college freshmen experiences major depression or a manic-depressive episode. Of course, this means four out of five go through the same stressful year without showing serious psychiatric symptoms. This suggests that stress can't be the only cause for what is commonly called a "nervous breakdown."

Harriet's case resembles Don's, in that Don lost his job, and low mood was a normal reaction. The main concern was that he didn't seem able to shake it. Harriet moved to a new city, then to college. Some degree of homesickness was to be expected. But in a person with a personality disorder, that amount of upheaval may trigger a longer-lasting depressive mood—and in someone with an inherited vulnerability to a mood disorder, it may cause major depression.

Dr. R.M.A. Hirschfield and colleagues looked for six years at 370 family members of patients with a major depressive disorder. As we learned in the previous chapter, these people were at higher-than-average risk for mood disorder. Twenty-nine persons, or eight percent experienced their first depressive episode during the six-year observation period. Among those older than 30 who got depressed, the typical personality profile showed decreased emotional strength, increased interpersonal dependency, and more thoughtfulness. It's reasonable to assume that people who have an inherited lack of emotional strength are at risk for both spontaneous and stress-induced depression.

BIOCHEMICAL VULNERABILITY

"Ever since she got her first menstrual period, Marsha has been much more depressed and moody than her sister ever was," this young woman's mother said. "I hope it won't be long before she finds the right man to marry. Maybe children and her own family will help her to get over her moods. But come to think of it, maybe she should wait awhile before she has kids. I remember how depressed I was for months after my first baby was born."

Marsha's depression associated with puberty, and her mother's depression associated with childbirth, point to a biochemical vulnerability—possibly heightened by the hormonal changes of first menstruation and childbirth. If Marsha sought help from a psychodynamically-oriented therapist who was not attuned to seeking physical causes, this biological aspect of the problem would probably have been overlooked. Long hours of therapy and much money might have been wasted on analyzing Marsha's "fears of becoming a woman."

Life events as true causes of clinical depression are rare. We need more prospective studies like Dr. Paula Clayton's which focused on people whose spouses had died unexpectedly. Many developed symptoms that looked like major depression, but none of them felt ill enough to consult a psychiatrist.

If you believe that psychodynamics reign supreme, you can always find psychological causes for your mental state. However, if you understand that psychic changes such as mood disturbances often occur as a result of genetically determined biochemical changes, you will be more sensitive to the complexity of psychic events.

The bottom line is: Major studies designed to evaluate the influences of both genetics and environment on psychiatric illness have *always* found genetic causes, and have *sometimes* also found environmental causes. The extent of the influence of the environment remains tantalizingly elusive. All we can say is that, so far, genetics can't explain everything.

BACK TO GENETICS

As we stated in the previous chapter, some research results suggest that it may take several genes to cause a severe manic-depressive disorder. But the severe disorder is relatively rare in the general population. The family histories of these patients show that some relatives may have much milder forms of the illness. Such people may be more vulnerable to environmentally triggered lows and highs.

At present there is no test that can pinpoint how large a role life events play in triggering episodes of mania or depression. Until recently, psychiatrists conceived of a fairly simple model. A person can be born with a genetic vulnerability to environmental influences. Place this vulnerable person in an unusual or stressful situation, and mania or depression may result.

But as we study more and more patients, our model is growing much more complicated. We identify a person as genetically vulnerable, so we watch him closely and see him coping adequately in quite a few stressful situations. Then, all of a sudden, the mood shift occurs. He's confronted with the same situation that he's dealt with ten times before, but this time it's too much for him.

Doctors have begun to redirect their attention from the outside to the inside, realizing that at times the chemical reaction in the body comes first. Body chemistry can heighten a person's sensitivity to both pleasure and pain. When a biochemical imbalance occurs, it may allow stress to trigger an outbreak of mania or depression.

AS TIME GOES BY

As he ages, the person with manic-depressive disorder often has episodes of unmanageable mood swings that last longer and occur closer together. With less "normal" time elapsing between episodes, it gets harder to point to an external cause for these mood shifts. Remember Martin in Chapter Three? He regarded the job he disliked, and the separation from his family, as the roots of his first depression. After recovery, he went through several years with mild symptoms. Martin's second major depressive episode was harder to attribute to life events, but he managed to chalk it up to getting older. What puzzled him was that he could no longer point to a single event that caused his depressed mood. Depression seemed to hit him "out of the blue."

"When I think I know the trigger these days," Martin tells us, "it's sometimes so ridiculous I'm ashamed to bring it up. I watch my oldest son playing with his daughter, for example, and then I recall that my first depression came when the kids were little. I didn't have time to play with them as much as I wanted to. It's almost as if I resent my son for having this time. Just thinking about fathers playing with their children gets me depressed. It's crazy."

As we've noted, sometimes when outside events are associated with depression or mania, it's actually the mood change that has made us more susceptible to what's going on around us.

DEPRESSION AND PATHOLOGICAL THOUGHTS

Renee, age 50, is tormented. She says, "I was cooking dinner last month, putting green beans in a pot, and suddenly I remembered when I was six years old and didn't want to eat my vegetables. I waited until my mother wasn't looking, and then I threw my beans to the dog." She pauses, "All of a sudden I realized that I've been paying for that incident ever since. That's the reason why I don't have enough energy now. I need to be punished for my disobedience. I'm going to be stuck this way forever. I even heard my mother's voice from the grave: 'Die for your sins.'"

Doug's wife tells us: "So I grabbed the kids and ran to a neighbor's. I just felt I had to get out of there before he hurt someone. I've never seen anything like it. Doug's been working hard. He was tired and a little down, we all knew that. So he took off work for a few days to rest up. Anyway, he's sitting around listening to tapes, relaxing, and all of a sudden I hear him screaming. Turns out he'd gone to play a record, and discovered the needle skipped. First thing he does is turn the controls every which way. Then he starts screaming at me and the kids, demanding to know if we'd ever touched the thing. And when we said no, he starts calling all the kids' friends, shouting into the phone, accusing them all of using it. I yelled at him to stop and he threw the phone at me, screaming, 'You planned this out. You want to drive me crazy. That's why you messed with the record player.' That's when I ran out."

In old movies, a character would slip on a banana peel and everyone would laugh. Often the reasons people give to explain their depression or rage seem just as petty as that banana peel.

There are also times, as Doug's wife found out, when depression and mania follow each other closely, with barely a pause for breath. While Renee's "green bean theory" may strike us as amusing, Doug's manic "record player rage" forces us to take sides with Doug's wife.

Renee's and Doug's problems are easy to understand. Anyone can see that what they call a *cause* is really a *symptom* of their disordered mood. Often, though, it's harder to be sure. Sympathetic friends and family frequently try hard to identify with the pain the other person feels.

Most roller coaster people find an activity or explanation that fits their mood. This is most evident when they attribute a good mood and, at another time, a bad mood to the *same event*.

THE SAME EVENT IN DIFFERENT LIGHTS

Gary had been flying high for the past six months. "When he came home and told me he'd been promoted at work," his wife said, "I thought it was the best thing that had ever happened to us. We've been married for fifteen years, and I'd never seen him so happy. More than just the extra money—though God knows we can use it—it was the idea that someone in the company was finally paying attention to all the extra hours Gary had been putting in, the extra effort he always made. Every weekend we'd go out to celebrate, the best restaurants, wine with dinner, nothing was too good for us. And he wasn't even tired when he got home from work. I don't know where he got all the energy. Sometimes we made love three times a night.

"Then all of a sudden, three months later, I'm sitting there on a Saturday night all dressed up, ready to go out to dinner, but Gary tells me he doesn't feel up to it. 'People expect too much from me,' he says—and the way he says it makes me feel like I'm one of those people! He tells me he's not sure he's going to be able to handle the extra pressure at work. Being sales manager is for the birds, he tells me—he wishes he could just go back to being an ordinary salesman. He says he was just fooling his boss and he got promoted for false reasons. After he'd been so excited about it just a few weeks before, I just didn't know what to say to him."

DEBBIE'S FLIP-FLOP

Debbie, December 14: "I think I'll wear my red velvet cape to the office Christmas party Saturday night, and the green dress. Men like fleshy women. I weigh 170 pounds and I love every inch of it. I don't mind letting people see my body, either. God, I love this low-cut dress, men will be dying to dance with me! And I'll dance with them all— married men and grandfathers included. I'll give them all a treat they'll never forget. I'll take them on two at a time if I have to. Come to Mama, honey."

Debbie, March 15: "I'm not in the mood to go to the St. Patrick's Day party. Tom only invited me to be kind, anyway. I know he doesn't really want me there. I've tried on three different dresses today. One of them didn't zip up all the way, and the other two don't hang right. I hate the way I look. Haven't washed my hair in two weeks, but what's the difference? No more parties. I'm not going to another party until I've lost forty pounds. No more parties, ever. Oh sure, sure, I can tell myself I'll diet, but I'm not going to stick to it this time either, I know I'm not. I'm just permanently fat, so I might as well get used to my 170 pounds of loneliness."

MOODS RULE MINDS

The playwright Eugene Ionesco once said: "It isn't what people think that's important, but the *reason* they think what they think." The manic-depressive person often drives and pushes himself, setting rigid rules and unattainable goals, then getting intensely self-critical when he can't reach those goals. When he's depressed, he's overly sensitive to other people's opinions. Minor obstacles loom like mountains. Temporary setbacks seem earth-shattering.

When people are going through a manic or depressed period, thoughts are often the "icing on the cake," the justifications they find to cap off the way they feel. Gary and Debbie are perfect examples. The *exact same* life experience— being promoted at work or being overweight—is viewed as the reason for being happy at one point, and down in the dumps a few months later.

Friends and family might remind Gary and Debbie of happier times, but neither one will remember those times. For both, the way they are now seems like the way they have always been. If there was ever happiness in their lives, they feel it was just a fluke. Depression makes them distort the past.

It's a waste of time to put patients like Gary and Debbie through prolonged psychotherapy to look for childhood traumas that might account for their severe mood swings. The biologically-oriented psychiatrist knows that the issues of job promotion and overweight are merely hooks on which Gary and Debbie hang their emotions. For a patient with a mood disturbance, it's much easier to point to an outside cause of a mood swing than to recognize a change from within.

Chapter 6

The Biochemistry
of Bipolar
Disorder

All of us have our moods. Some days we wake up in the morning with the feeling we can do no wrong. Other days, well . . . we get up "on the wrong side of the bed." We burn our fingers on the coffee pot, spill the juice, scorch the toast, and curse at the traffic jam on our way to work. We realize we're in a bad mood, but we usually don't stop to consider the role body chemistry plays in producing those moods.

LIKE CLOCKWORK

Each of us has a personal body clock, to which we adjust and adapt quite early in life. Jim, a computer programmer, works beautifully at daybreak, but after about two o'clock in the afternoon he's not very productive. He has learned to get to the office early in the morning. By the time his colleagues show up at their desks, Jim has already accomplished a lot.

Shirley, an author, is the opposite. "My friends know not to call in the morning if they want to stay friends," she says. "At ten A.M., I'm likely to bite their head off." Shirley routinely stays up working past midnight. She has always felt best after sundown. That's when she gets most of her writing done.

Jim is a lark; Shirley, an owl. We know it's their body clocks that regulate their moods and activity levels.

TIME FLIES

Our pattern of sleeping and waking sets the pace for the body's metabolism, which in turn regulates body temperature, bowel function, circulation of the blood, and many other mechanisms. Lose a night's sleep, and the entire system is somewhat disrupted. Lose three nights' sleep in a row, and it gets harder and harder to function.

Similarly, when we fly from California to New York, we experience "jet lag," which throws the body system off balance. Dinner is served at six P.M., but we're not hungry because our body, still working on Pacific Time, "knows" it's only three o'clock in the afternoon. Some of us even have trouble adjusting when we set the clock forward an hour in spring and back an hour in autumn.

BROKEN CLOCKS

An early discovery in biological psychiatry was the link between depression and changing sleep patterns. A person in a classic depression has trouble falling asleep and trouble staying asleep—particularly during the early morning hours. A person experiencing a period of mania requires only a few hours of sleep each night. Why? The answer, according to one theory, involves two clocks that govern our lives.

The strong biological clock, which controls many of our physical functions, causes our body temperature to peak at about four P.M. That's when our reaction time is shortest and we can reach our peak performance. Subsequently, body temperature begins a gradual drop, reaching its lowest point at about four A.M.—no time to try to win a tennis match, for most people. From that point, our temperature rises again and our adrenal glands secrete more cortisol, getting us ready for the next day's work and play.

In addition to this biological clock, most of us follow a social clock: activity during the day and rest during the night. If we wish, we can occasionally ignore this clock, dancing far into the night or watching TV until early morning. We can usually get away with this for a night or so, catching up on lost sleep later.

Overall, our biological and social clocks run in sync. But in depression, the biological clock runs faster. Body temperature reaches its lowest point earlier in the night—let's say at two A.M. instead of four A.M.—and cortisol production starts earlier. These events cause early morning awakening—one of the classic symptoms of biological depression.

As Dr. Ronald R. Fieve pointed out in his book *Moodswing*, part of the secret of those sanatorium rest cures doctors recommended a hundred years ago was simply forced rest. The daily schedule nudged the body clock back into a "regular" schedule of sleeping and eating.

NEW-MODEL SANATORIUMS

In the old days, a patient who entered a sanatorium stayed there for several months, letting the body cycle readjust at its own rather leisurely rate. Today, medical research and new medications have made it possible for doctors to speed up the readjustment process.

In research experiments, depressed patients felt better when they dramatically changed their sleep-wake cycle—for example, going to sleep at five P.M. and waking at two A.M. Medications such as lithium and MAO inhibitors may produce similar alterations in the body's *circadian* (daily) *rhythm*. We talk more about medication effects in Chapter Seven.

PMS AND MOOD SWINGS

Many women become depressed or irritable around the time of menstruation. One psychoanalytic theory, now outmoded, held that menstruation-linked suffering betrayed a woman's refusal to accept her sexuality.

Over the past two decades it's been found that in many women, the moodiness of the premenstrual and early menstrual period—*premenstrual syndrome, PMS*— is due to the cyclical hormonal and endocrine changes that the female body undergoes. These changes may cause stronger reactions in women who are genetically susceptible to mild manic-depressive disorder. In one study, two-thirds of the women diagnosed with PMS had family histories of either unipolar or bipolar disorder. If you experience mood swings just before the onset of menses, you may have a biochemical imbalance that medication can help correct.

BIOCHEMICAL PATHWAYS

The body's genes determine hormonal secretion into the bloodstream, and excitatory and inhibitory biochemical activity in the nervous system. These electro-biochemical circuitries or systems are closely linked with the body's circadian rhythm and with moods.

If the precise chemical imbalance in the nervous system can be found, it can often be corrected with medications (see the following "Brain Boosters" box). But diagnosing the imbalance and choosing the appropriate medication is no simple undertaking.

Tests of neurotransmitter function have been developed over the past ten years; research scientists are still in the process of refining them. The test results can help physicians diagnose and treat a patient's condition. However, since test results are not foolproof, they never provide the sole basis for a diagnosis. Rather, they help make the psychiatrist's assessment as complete as possible.

NERVES, GLANDS, AND BLOOD

The neurotransmitter systems that affect mood also control the body's endocrine glands; clinicians call this whole package the *neuroendocrine system*. In mood disorders, the neuroendocrine system may be disturbed, which is why we speak of a "biochemical imbalance" in the body. As we will now see, the degree of neuroendocrine malfunction can be measured by studying blood samples.

Three endocrine glands are particularly interesting to psychiatrists because of their effect on mood: the *thyroid gland*, which lies in front of the throat and secretes thyroid hormone; the *adrenal glands*, which sit like caps on the kidneys and secrete several hormones including cortisol; and finally the *pituitary gland,* an appendix-like structure at the base of the brain, which acts as the body's master gland.

BRAIN BOOSTERS

At least three biochemical systems in the brain regulate mood. The first one secretes *dopamine,* the second, *norepinephrine,* and the third, *serotonin;* thus these three systems are called the dopaminergic, noradrenergic, and serotonergic systems. The secreted chemicals transmit information—by means of on-off "switches," somewhat in the manner of a computer—to neighboring neurons (nerve cells). For this reason, these chemicals are called neurotransmitters.

Neurotransmitters are composed of amino acids—building blocks formed from proteins that we get from the foods we eat. *Tyrosine,* one of the amino acids, is transformed in the brain cells into dopamine and norepinephrine. *Tryptophane,* another amino acid, is transformed into serotonin.

Research scientists believe that depression may involve an undersupply, and mania an oversupply, of one or more of these three key neurotransmitters.

The anterior frontal lobe of the pituitary traps blood coming from the hypothalamus of the brain. This blood contains "releasing factors," which tell the pituitary which hormones when to release, and in what amounts.

YOU AND YOUR THYROID

The thyroid functions in concert with the hypothalamus and the pituitary gland. In the brain, the hypothalamus secretes thyrotropin-releasing hormone (TRH), which stimulates the pituitary to release thyroid-stimulating hormone (known as TSH or thyrotropin). TSH stimulates the thyroid to release thyroid hormones into the bloodstream. Levels of thyroid hormone in the blood regulate the pituitary's continued release of TSH. This feedback mechanism switches off the pituitary if the thyroid hormone level rises too high, and makes the pituitary pump out more TSH if the thyroid hormone level falls below normal. In thyroid disorders, the thyroid gland goes off-system, secreting its hormones against pituitary commands.

THE TRH STIMULATION TEST IN DEPRESSION

The TRH stimulation test for depression looks beyond the level of thyroid hormones in the blood, examining a chain of endocrine glands and hormones that activate one another: the hypothalamus, which secretes thyroid-releasing hormone (TRH); the pituitary, which secretes thyroid-stimulating hormone (TSH); and the thyroid gland, which secretes thyroid hormones T3 and T4. First, a blood sample is taken to determine the patient's present TSH level. Then a dose of artificial TRH hormone is administered. Blood is drawn again 15, 30, and 90 minutes later, and TSH levels are measured.

If the person's thyroid system is functioning normally, the TSH level rises slightly within an hour to maintain normal equilibrium. But if the patient is depressed, the response is blunted: very little TSH is secreted in response to the dose of artificial TRH. Approximately 40 percent of depressed patients respond sluggishly to TRH.

NEUROTRANSMITTERS, TRH, AND DEPRESSION

Dopamine and norepinephrine increase production of TRH (thyroid-releasing hormone), and serotonin inhibits it. Proof is still lacking, but it's thought that in some types of depression serotonin is in short supply and thus can't inhibit TRH. Uninhibited TRH stimulation may desensitize the cells in the pituitary that release TSH. This would explain the sluggish response of the pituitary in a depressed patient who is given an injection of TRH.

THE DEXAMETHASONE SUPPRESSION TEST

Another hormone-based diagnostic test for depression is the dexamethasone suppression test. It uses a synthetic hydrocortisone hormone, dexamethasone, to test the response of the body's cortisol production. Cortisol, a hormone controlled by the pituitary and adrenal glands, helps metabolize carbohydrates, fats, and proteins, and also regulates the body's response to stress. The patient with major depression appears overstressed. Therefore, he may have an abnormally high level of cortisol circulating.

In the dexamethasone suppression test, the patient takes a small white 1 mg tablet of dexamethasone at eleven P.M. The next day, a technician draws a blood sample at four P.M. and again at eleven P.M. In a nondepressed person the dose of dexamethasone will suppress the body's natural cortisol secretion, resulting in a cortisol level of less than four mg/dl. This suppression will continue for more than a day. In someone with major depression, the dose of dexamethasone supposedly suppresses the body's natural hormone production for only a few hours, resulting in a nonsuppressed blood cortisol level 17 and 24 hours later.

The dexamethasone suppression test is useful for detecting both unipolar depression and bipolar disorders. However, endocrine abnormalities are found in less than half of all people with manic-depressive illness or major depression. This is why other tests, such as the insulin-growth hormone challenge test, are also used in making a diagnosis.

NEUROTRANSMITTERS, DEXAMETHASONE, AND DEPRESSION

Norepinephrine inhibits the release of the hormone cortisol, and serotonin stimulates it. In depression, cortisol levels tend to be high, which may indicate a shortage of norepinephrine in the brain. We assume that different depressions are associated with lacks of different neurotransmitters. How can we distinguish one kind of depression from another? Since dexamethasone does nothing to interfere with possible overstimulation by serotonin, a positive response to the dexamethasone suppression test suggests that the patient's depression is caused by a shortage of norepinephrine, rather than a shortage of serotonin. This knowledge helps the physician choose an antidepressant medication that will be effective.

THE INSULIN-GROWTH HORMONE
CHALLENGE TEST

In the healthy person, an insulin injection stimulates indirectly the pituitary gland to release growth hormone. This response is noticeably blunted in some depressed patients.

Clinical and research psychiatrists are trying to assemble a battery of hormone tests that will detect and distinguish among the various types of depression. A complete battery would help doctors diagnose patients whose symptom patterns are unclear or unusual. It would be particularly useful to the clinician treating children and teens with conduct and behavior disorders, since it's suspected that some of these young people suffer from unrecognized forms of depression or bipolar illness.

MEASURING THE LITHIUM RATIO

From 70 to 80 percent of patients with manic-depressive disorder respond favorably to lithium salt (more on this in Chapter Seven): their manic but less so their depressive episodes become fewer and milder, and may disappear altogether.

Lithium penetrates the cell walls of the body, reaching a concentration within the cell that is usually lower than its concentration in the blood. The body cells of people with manic-depressive illness seem to be inefficient at pumping lithium back into the bloodstream. In these people, therefore, the ratio of lithium-in-the-cells to lithium-in-the-blood is abnormally high. To determine this ratio in a given patient, psychiatrists draw a small blood sample. A laboratory technician spins down the blood in a centrifuge, separating the clear plasma from the blood-cell sediment. Then he measures the lithium concentration in the packed red blood cells, and compares it to the plasma lithium concentration.

Typical lithium ratios in patients with manic-depressive disorder are .55 (females) and .50 (males), versus .35 for healthy people. In unipolar depressed patients, typical lithium ratios fall somewhere in between the bipolar and the normal values.

While the lithium ratio test can be useful in diagnosing a manic-depressive disorder, it does not predict if the patient will respond to treatment with lithium medication.

NEUROTRANSMITTER PATHWAYS

A nerve cell (neuron) generates an electrical signal that travels down the axon, an elongated part of the cell. This electrical signal cannot reach the next nerve cell all by itself, since gaps called synapses separate nerve cells from one another. How does the electrical signal bridge the gap? By freeing a special chemical—a *neurotransmitter*—as soon as it reaches the synapse. This neurotransmitter travels across the synapse to the next nerve cell and finds a sensitive spot into which it fits, just as a key fits into a keyhole. The sensitive spot, or "keyhole," is called a *receptor*. Stimulated by the arrival of the neurotransmitter, the receptor in turn generates a new electrical signal. Certain nerve cells associated with specific neurotransmitters constitute a neurotransmitter pathway or system (see "Brain Boosters" box on page 82).

TESTING NEUROTRANSMITTER PATHWAYS

The three neurotransmitters crucial to mood—norepinephrine, serotonin, and dopamine—can be released by specific medications. These medications are thus used diagnostically to test the strength or weakness of the neurotransmitter pathways. If the pathway is weak, a medication "challenge" (administration of a single dose of an appropriate medication) will stimulate release of the neurotransmitter, temporarily relieving the depression.

It's thought that too much dopamine may cause the hypermobility and psychotic behavior sometimes seen in mania, since dopamine speeds up the brain's chemical reactions. Antipsychotic medications, which reduce dopamine levels, are often used to calm down a manic patient.

Norepinephrine and serotonin both work to keep a person from getting too "high" (manic) or too depressed. Thus, insufficient levels of these neurotransmitters may cause depression, and excessive levels may result in anxiety or mania. Antidepressant medications work by adjusting these levels.

THE DEXTROAMPHETAMINE CHALLENGE

Dextroamphetamine (Dexedrine) is a stimulant medication that increases a person's pulse rate, blood pressure, respiration, body temperature, perspiration, and other metabolic functions. In particular, Dexedrine modifies the norepinephrine and dopamine functions, stimulating nerve impulses and body movements and heightening the person's awareness of his "nervous energy." In the Dexedrine challenge test, we give the patient 10 to 20 milligrams of Dexedrine, then use standardized rating scales to monitor his response over the next four hours.

SIX RESPONSES TO DEXEDRINE

Number 1: "My kids want me to take them to a rock concert this weekend," says Drew. "I hate rock music, but I'm afraid to let them go alone. Meanwhile, Ellen's screaming at me that if I don't start spending more time with her she's going to buck out of the relationship. All I feel like doing is crawling into bed and not seeing anyone till I have to go to work on Monday," Drew says. He has been depressed for close to a month now, and he can't seem to pull himself out of it.

As we are talking, he begins to respond to the Dexedrine. He doesn't feel quite as depressed now, so he begins to reason a little better. "I guess I really do want to be with the kids this weekend," he says. "It's just that damn concert that gets to me. Maybe I'll take them to a movie or something. If Ellen wants to come along, that's up to her."

While we're talking, Drew's depression continues to lift. He feels more cheerful, but he doesn't become excited or show other signs of mania. He is suffering from a unipolar depression, which may respond to medication that increases norepinephrine and possibly dopamine in certain brain synapses.

Number 2: "Let me out of here, I've got to get the hell out of here," Anne screams. She runs to the door, but can't get it open because her hands are sweating. "You locked it, you bastard! You're trying to keep me here. I've got to get out!" A half hour after taking Dexedrine, Anne begins to sweat. She complains of chest pain and breathing trouble, and she starts to hyperventilate.

The diagnostic picture becomes clear: in Anne, the small amount of Dexedrine has triggered a panic attack. Anne is 15 years old and has never panicked before. We suspect she may have an underlying anxiety disorder instead of, or in addition to, depression.

Number 3: Ten-year-old Timmy was previously diagnosed as having attention-deficit hyperactivity disorder (ADHD). After receiving a challenge dose of Dexedrine, he is observed in the hospital playroom. He has been riding one of the bikes all morning, but now an attendant intercepts him seconds before he crashes into the wall. "Let me go," Timmy screams. The aide tells him that he'll hurt himself. "No I won't. Nothing can hurt me." Timmy is convinced that the wall is only there for other people—that he can ride right through it, spin the bike around in the air, and ride back in without being hurt. It's as we expected: Dexedrine has pushed Timmy into a state of mania that isn't typical of ADHD. His "grandiosity" (heightened sense of his own power) is a sign of bipolar disorder.

Number 4: Eight-year-old Randy is a terror on the children's unit. He hits other kids, kicks and spits at the nurses, and refuses to take "time out" as a punishment. He leaves his room when he's asked to stay there for ten minutes. He can't attend to any schoolwork; he gets up, roams around, and disrupts the class. He even has trouble sitting still to watch TV. Randy is suffering from attention-deficit hyperactivity disorder (ADHD).

The Dexedrine challenge test made a big difference. An hour after swallowing the tablet, Randy sat still for his evaluation, answering questions without playing with his shoelaces. He started a page in his coloring book, and had nearly finished it by the time we rated him. Under the influence of Dexedrine, Randy could pay attention. During the second hour he went to the hospital school, and surprised his teacher by attending to task. He stayed in his seat, copied words from the board, and even told two other students to sit still and leave him alone. Dexedrine, although technically a stimulant, had the paradoxical effect of reversing Randy's hyperactivity.

Since the Dexedrine test was positive, we expected that the medication imipramine, alone or combined with a little Dexedrine or methylphenidate (Ritalin), would help Randy handle school and get along with his peers and teachers.

Number 5: Jack, 62, sits alone in the corner of his room. His movements are slow, almost imperceptible. He doesn't look at the doctor examining him, and he doesn't answer any questions. In clinical terms, Jack is mute and has severe psychomotor retardation. His present state is sometimes called *catatonia*. Is Jack demented? Does he know who and where he is? Is he frightened because he hears voices? His blood pressure, pulse, and electrocardiogram are all normal. We give him the Dexedrine challenge test.

Slowly Jack swallows the four 5 mg tablets. After half an hour he looks up, and when the doctor asks questions he nods or shakes his head in answer. Then he begins to speak in a low voice. Finally, after an hour and a half, he tells us he's afraid someone will poison him because he killed Jesus Christ. He's hearing voices that tell him he has to die.

Yet Jack knows the name of the hospital, the day of the week, and even the first name of one of the nurses. After another ten minutes, he can repeat the examining doctor's name. Thus, he's not severely demented. He is suffering from a psychosis—most likely psychotic depression. Besides a tricyclic antidepressant, Jack may need an antipsychotic medication that will stop his delusional thoughts and keep him from hearing voices.

Number 6: Vicki, a 32-year-old secretary, has taken time off from work to undergo the Dexedrine challenge test.

When she arrives at the office she's tense, nervous, irritable, and depressed. Three hours later, she's still waiting for something to happen. She says there has been no change in her mood, and certainly she doesn't seem any more cheerful or sociable. The test result is negative. Only 40 percent of patients like Vicki are helped by taking a tricyclic antidepressant. By contrast, 90 percent of the patients like Drew, who become more assertive and cheerful after taking Dexedrine, respond well to tricyclic antidepressants.

THE FENFLURAMINE CHALLENGE

We then performed another diagnostic test on Vicki: the fenfluramine (Pondimin) challenge test. Patients who don't respond to the Dexedrine challenge test may cheer up rapidly when we administer 60 milligrams of the medication fenfluramine. You'll recall that at least three neurotransmitter systems regulate mood. Whereas Dexedrine affects the norepinephine and dopamine systems, fenfluramine affects the serotonin system, releasing serotonin from the cells and into the synapses where it attaches to the serotonin receptors of neighboring cells.

If Vicki were suffering from panic disorder, fenfluramine might have spurred a panic attack. Instead, she calmed down and told us she hadn't felt so well in weeks. "It's as if I'd been carrying around a sack of rocks, and suddenly someone took it away from me," she said. And in a sense, that's what had happened. Vicki's serotonergic nerve cells did not release enough serotonin; the imbalance between the serotonin and norepinephrine pathways in her brain had made her irritable and tense. When fenfluramine caused a release of serotonin, her tension suddenly subsided. This test result suggested that Vicki could be treated with medications that increase serotonin in the synapses between brain cells. These include fluoxetine (Prozac) and trazodone (Desyrel).

Although a number of investigators have studied the Dexedrine challenge test, the fenfluramine test has so far had only one empirical evaluation, by Dr. Steven Targum. We always use it in conjunction with the Dexedrine challenge test—usually on people who don't respond to Dexedrine. To date, we don't know if the fenfluramine challenge test has high predictive power. We think it's worthwhile, however, since it may save some patients four to six weeks of hospital treatment.

The Dexedrine challenge test isolates two neurotransmitter systems, and the fenfluramine challenge test may predict a response in the third. The reality of mood disorders, however, is more complicated than this might suggest. Present knowledge suggests that all three mood-related neurotransmitter systems *interact* to produce the highs and lows of a manic-depressive disorder.

THIS IS NOT ALL

With many patients, the tests just described, used separately or in combination, can help diagnose an affective disorder and may predict the patient's response to various treatments. Another diagnostic aid is the measurement of 3-methoxy-4-hydroxyphenylglycol (MHPG) in the urine and, more recently, in the blood. Since MHPG is a waste product of norepinephrine, a high concentration of it indicates an abundance of norepinephrine, and a low concentration suggests a shortage. A patient with a low MHPG level—and thus, presumably, a shortage of norepinephrine—would be expected to have a positive reaction to the Dexedrine challenge test.

Several investigators have measured MHPG concentrations in urine samples collected over 24 hours. Bipolar depressed patients were found to have the lowest MHPG values. Patients with less than 1,950 micrograms of MHPG per 24 hours tend to be helped by antidepressant medication that increases norepinephrine in the brain, such as desipramine (Norpramine) and maprotiline (Ludiomil).

Many more tests now being performed experimentally may enter the diagnostic process in the near future, making chemical imbalances easier to define, pinpoint, and correct. As in any medical condition, proper diagnosis of a mood disorder is the first and most important step toward successful treatment.

Chapter 7

Medication: Getting Back on Track

IT DOESN'T HAVE TO BE THAT WAY

If you have mood swings, even relatively mild mood swings, you don't have to suffer any more: there are medications that can help you. *With proper treatment, 70 to 80 percent of patients with mood swings can experience a partial to complete remission of their symptoms*. The other 20 to 30 percent may remain somewhat moody, depressed, shy, or socially awkward, but their symptoms may be far less severe than before.

"Psychiatric disorders are brain disorders," Wilhelm Griesinger said back in 1845. He was right: biological psychiatry *does* begin in the brain. Medical research is finding more and more evidence of brain-based chemical imbalances that result in psychiatric illness.

But to what extent do genes determine our destiny? Are psychiatric conditions inevitable? Are we all just "playing the hand we were dealt?"

The answer seems to be: genes play an important role, but we're learning to counter their negative effects. By adjusting the brain's chemistry and altering its reactions, we can treat psychiatric disorders—and thus combat genetic predispositions.

Psychopharmacology—the science of using medication to improve brain function—includes both old and new remedies. Since the early 1950s, medical scientists have been introducing new medications and improving available remedies such as stimulants, sedatives, hypnotics, narcotics, and electroconvulsive therapy. Over the last three decades we have also learned much about dosage and side effects. The net result is treatment that's increasingly effective.

THE PSYCHIATRIST AS CLINICIAN

"Choosing the most suitable antidepressant for a particular patient is still more of an art than a science," according to doctors Donald W. Goodwin and Samuel B. Guze. This doesn't mean a psychiatrist prescribes whimsically. Rather, it means that his choice of medication will depend on his evaluation of diverse factors: how physically healthy, intelligent, and mature the patient is, how strong his social support system is, and whether he has suicidal tendencies.

Choosing the right medication involves more than diagnostic tests. It also includes understanding what the patient wants from treatment, and which side effects he is willing to tolerate.

Choosing medication for a patient with bipolar disorder may be particularly tricky because symptoms change so quickly. Some manic-depressive people spend little time being normal— they're always on their way up or down. An excited bipolar patient, especially with hallucinations, might need an antipsychotic medication to calm him down quickly. Later he might be switched to lithium treatment to prevent relapses.

Here are brief descriptions of the most common and effective medications for bipolar disorder.

LITHIUM: MANIC-DEPRESSIVE DISORDER'S WONDER DRUG

If the patient is experiencing mania, hypomania (which threatens to impair his judgment), or rapid mood swings, the psychiatrist's first choice of medication will most likely be lithium.

Lithium's role in treating affective illness has been known since the early 1900s, when it was used to treat melancholia. It was rediscovered serendipitously in 1949 by the Australian researcher John F. Cade, who was searching for substances that might cause psychiatric disorders. Cade injected the urine of mental patients into guinea pigs. To help them absorb it, he also injected lithium urate. To his surprise, he noted that the animals became sluggish. Cade concluded that lithium might be useful in treating mental illness.

But for many years his idea lay dormant, because in the 1950s American psychiatry was dominated by psychodynamic thinking. Most psychiatrists had ignored Freud's notion that psychiatric disorders might arise from chemical imbalances—imbalances that could respond to medication. Consequently, lithium did not receive official approval by the Food and Drug Administration until 1969—a full twenty years after Cade's discovery. Today, many people with manic-depressive disorder, who previously would have been condemned to an unending roller coaster ride, can now live virtually symptom-free.

Usually the bipolar patient requires a long-term lithium maintenance schedule. In other words, he has to keep on taking lithium indefinitely, day in, day out. When taken over an extended period, lithium prevents or minimizes future episodes of mood swing. In a recent study of patients whose manic-depressive disorder was considered to be temporarily in remission, it was found that 61 percent of the patients *not* maintained on lithium still had some residual symptoms of the illness between episodes. In contrast, all of the patients who were maintained on lithium were as well between episodes as people in a control group who had no history of psychiatric illness. Moreover, even when the lithium-maintained patients did have manic or depressive periods, these periods were less severe and less frequent than before lithium was given.

The lithium dosage is adjusted until the patient's mood stabilizes. As he grows older he may need a lower dosage. Why is this? Lithium is water-soluble, which means it dissolves in the water of the body. An older person's body tends to contain less water—so if he is taking lithium, the lithium in his body becomes more concentrated. Lowering the dosage keeps the lithium concentration stable.

DON'T STOP LITHIUM!

If you're taking lithium, don't go off it without consulting your psychiatrist—the results can be disastrous! One study my wife and I conducted in Kansas City involved patients with bipolar disorder who had inadequate responses to, or severe side effects from, lithium. These patients, who had signed up to try bupropion (Wellbutrin) as a possible alternative medication, stopped taking lithium for a while before starting the new medicine. Within six weeks, 50 percent of them had a manic episode. Other researchers had similar experiences. Patients who stop taking lithium without their physician's supervision risk a catastrophic resurgence of their illness.

Before placing any patient on a long-term medication, both the psychiatrist and the patient usually explore all the benefits, limitations, and risks. While lithium remains the medication of choice for treating mania, people whose mood swings are moderate may be able to control their disorder without medication—for instance, through cognitive therapy and relaxation techniques. If past episodes of mania or depression were infrequent, the psychiatrist may recommend treating acute episodes with medications other than lithium.

LITHIUM'S DOWNSIDE

Lithium, which is given as a salt—either lithium carbonate or lithium citrate—has various side effects. Some surface within days or weeks, others after several months or even later. In 1948, lithium chloride, used unrestrictedly as a salt substitute, had caused some death in the U.S., signaling the fatal danger of overdose.

In therapeutic dosages, Lithium can cause thirst and frequent urination. It can irritate the stomach wall, producing some discomfort. It can cause diarrhea.

Lithium also increases what's known as essential tremor. All people have a tremor in their hands—to see the proof, just put a piece of construction paper over your outstretched hand and watch the paper tremble slightly. To varying degrees, lithium makes this tremor more pronounced.

Ways to deal with lithium side effects include reducing the dosage, allowing the body time to adjust, and giving other medications (propranolol) to treat the adverse effects.

Some side effects occur later. For instance, lithium can reduce thyroid function. About 10 percent of patients who take lithium require supplemental thyroid hormone.

Water retention and weight gain are other possible side effects. Some lithium-treated patients experience a craving for sweets, and end up eating a lot of candy bars or ice cream.

Thickening of the kidney membrane has been seen in kidney biopsies of people who took lithium for many years. However, these patients had normal kidney function. Patients rarely, *if ever,* require dialysis because of long-term lithium therapy. Some people have been on lithium for thirty years.

Do you remember the 72-year-old woman we mentioned in Chapter One, the one whose brother was worried about her? Without consulting her physician, she stopped taking lithium because she had gained weight. But once she was off medication, the manic-depressive symptoms returned. Her failure to consult her physician was unfortunate, because there were at least two possible alternatives: (1) continue taking lithium and lose weight through diet and exercise; or (2) try a different medication that would not cause weight gain.

Some psychiatrists have been treating female patients with carbamazepine (Tegretol) as first drug of choice because it's less likely to cause weight gain.

Another medication that may be tried if lithium causes excessive weight gain is clonazepam (Klonopin), a benzodiazepene which is often used as an anticonvulsant. To date, however, there is no firm evidence that Klonopin controls mood swings as effectively as lithium.

WHEN LITHIUM IS NOT ENOUGH:
TREATING ACUTE MANIA

Since lithium usually takes from ten days to two weeks to start working, it's of little use in acute manic episodes. In the short-term treatment of acute mania, *antipsychotic* medications give immediate relief. These medications work directly on the brain's *amine neurotransmitter system*, blocking brain receptors for *dopamine*.

ANXIETY OR HYPOMANIA?

When a wound-up hypomanic person consults his family doctor, the symptoms he describes may sound like anxiety. The general practitioner may therefore prescribe an antianxiety medication—a benzodiazepine such as diazepam (Valium) or alprazolam (Xanax).

Benzodiazepines do alleviate anxiety and panic. But with the exception of clonazepam, they do *not* ease hypomanic symptoms, and may in fact do the bipolar patient more harm than good. If such a patient still feels anxious (manic, actually) after taking a benzodiazepine, his impaired judgment may cause him to take another pill, and yet another—ignoring the recommended dosage in the hope that just a little more medicine will calm him down. In his still-anxious state, he may not remember how many pills he's taken—or the medication itself may disrupt his memory. With his reaction time slowed by excessive medication, he may be at increased risk for an auto accident. If he keeps popping pills to "get mellow," he may eventually become dependent on the medication.

Receptors recognize and receive chemical messengers from other nerve cells. Dopamine, one of these chemical messengers (neurotransmitters), stimulates brain function and physical activity. In mania, according to current thought, either too much dopamine is secreted or else the dopamine receptors are oversensitive. Using antipsychotic medication to block the receptors robs dopamine of its target, putting an end to overstimulation. When the dopamine level—or receptor sensitivity—returns to normal, the patient is less prone to mania or hallucinations.

Common first-choice antipsychotic medications are chlorpromazine (Thorazine) and haloperidol (Haldol). Either one can be taken orally or by injection—an injection may be necessary for a hospitalized patient who is severely manic and uncooperative. Another antipsychotic, thioridazine (Mellaril), can only be taken by mouth.

When antipsychotic medications are necessary, I usually prescribe them for brief periods, preferably for hospitalized patients. Over the short term they can be administered safely, although side effects may be bothersome. In some patients, the antipsychotics cause muscle pulling (dystonia), restlessness and a need to pace (akathisia), or tremors, stiffness, and poor coordination (Parkinsonism). They often interfere with a patient's ability to think clearly.

Over the long term, antipsychotic medications can cause tardive dyskinesia, a condition that may start as ceaseless chewing motions and later develop into uncontrollable twitches and spasms. Tardive dyskinesia may not go away even when the patient stops taking the medication. That's why we limit our use of antipsychotics to short-term treatment in most mood disorders.

WHEN LITHIUM IS NOT ENOUGH: TREATING NONRESPONDERS

Lithium, used alone, helps between 70 and 80 percent of bipolar patients. What about the other 20 to 30 percent? For unknown reasons, some patients have only a partial response to lithium—their mania decreases but does not disappear. Others have no response at all.

Some of these patients may simply need more lithium. Even if the psychiatrist monitors the patient's blood lithium level to make sure the dosage is adequate, blood levels don't always predict the brain's response. For some nonresponding patients whose blood lithium levels seem adequate, we may try increasing the lithium dosage anyway. Of course, we closely monitor the patient's response.

If there's no change for the better even at the higher dosage, we may switch the patient to a different medication, or add a second medication to the lithium regimen.

Auxiliary or alternative medications we consider are *anticonvulsants* (seizure medications) such as carbamazepine (Tegretol), clonazepam (Klonopin), and valproic acid (Depakote). Carbamazepine, which is chemically related to the tricyclic antidepressants, is the one we use most often. It seems to slow down overly excitable nerve cells, making manic episodes less likely. One study found that half the patients who didn't respond well to lithium improved dramatically when they took a combination of lithium and carbamazepine.

Relatively new medications that may also work well with lithium are verapamil (Calan, Isoptin) and other *calcium channel blockers,* which slow down the normal flow of calcium into the cells. Calcium influx is essential for the release of dopamine and norepinephrine into the synapse. As we saw earlier, manic-depressive patients are thought to have either an oversupply of dopamine and norepinephrine, or else overly sensitive receptors for these two neurotransmitters; calcium channel blockers reduce that oversupply. Although the calcium channel blockers are most often used to treat high blood pressure and heart conditions, they may also help attenuate mood swings in some patients.

WHEN LITHIUM IS NOT ENOUGH: TREATING DEPRESSION

Lithium works most effectively against mania. It may also help relieve a bipolar patient's depression (remember that its first use, in the early 1900s, was for "melancholia"), but more potent antidepressant medication is often needed.

If a person with a bipolar illness seeks treatment for depression, the psychiatrist may first prescribe an antidepressant, then stop the antidepressant six to twelve months after his depression lifts, and monitor him closely for signs of mania or of recurring depression. His patient may then remain medication-free for a number of years.

If the patient has occasional bouts of mania, the physician may simply treat each episode with antipsychotic medication. His patient will be at higher risk for relapse than if he were on continuous lithium treatment, but he may prefer to take a chance rather than stay on medication indefinitely.

If he has frequent depressive episodes, it may be best to give him antidepressant medication initially, and later add lithium to prevent both manic and depressive episodes. For some patients, lithium enhances the effect of the antidepressant.

However, other patients who are first treated with a combination of lithium and an antidepressant never completely overcome their depression. If lithium is cut back or eliminated, the depression may lift, only to give way to a manic episode. Therefore, all the important treatment decisions must be made on an individual, case-by-case basis.

SELECTING AN ANTIDEPRESSANT

Four types of antidepressant medication are useful in treating patients with bipolar disorder: *tricyclic antidepressants, monoamine oxidase (MAO) inhibitors,* and two groups of recently approved medications that affect the serotonin (fluoxetine, trazodone) or presumably dopamine system (bupropion) respectively.

Although the tricyclics, which are most widely used, are the antidepressants of first choice, they are not perfect. For one thing, a tricyclic antidepressant may take three weeks or more to reach full effect—and for a depressed person, three weeks can seem like an eternity. For another, there is a 20 to 30 percent chance that the medication won't have any effect, even after a month or more of treatment. Fortunately, there are ways to predict a patient's response to certain medications.

Let's return to the two challenge tests, described in Chapter Six, which help predict treatment response. You may remember Vicki, who showed little response to the Dexedrine challenge test. After receiving a fenfluramine (Pondimin) challenge dose, Vicki said she hadn't felt so good in weeks. Her reactions to these two tests suggest that she may respond best to an antidepressant that works on the serotonin system, such as trazodone (Desyrel) or fluoxetine (Prozac); there's only a 40 percent chance she'll respond well to a tricyclic antidepressant. Timmy, who became manic in response to the Dexedrine challenge test, probably has a chemical imbalance involving norepinephrine and dopamine. There's an 80-90 percent chance that Timmy will respond to one of the tricyclic or tetracyclic (maprotiline, Ludiomil) antidepressants, which work directly on noradrenergic pathways of the brain. Since Dexedrine releases both norepinephrine and dopamine, the 10% Dexedrine responsive but tricyclic nonresponsive patients may respond to bupropion (Wellbutrin) which may enhance the dopaminergic system.

All tricyclic or tetracyclic antidepressants are about equally effective. How, then, do we choose among them? We base our decision on the potential side effects of the various medications. If our depressed patient is anxious and agitated, we prescribe a sedating antidepressant such as amitriptyline (Elavil or Endep), doxepin (Sinequan or Adapin), or trimipramine (Surmontil). If he is overly tired and lethargic, we choose a less sedating medication such as desipramine (Norpramin or Pertofrane), nortriptyline (Pamelor, Aventyl), or protriptyline (Vivactil).

TRIGGERING MANIA?

Many psychiatrists believe that a manic-depressive person who takes a tricyclic antidepressant alone (i.e., without auxiliary medication) is at risk for developing a manic episode. According to Dr. Frederick K. Goodwin, "Over 50 percent of the bipolar patients treated with tricyclics for depression develop more rapid cycles of their illness, and lithium alone does not always prevent this. Although the patient recovers from the depression quickly, the next mania also develops more quickly." Research is needed to explore this notion thoroughly.

Vivactil is the least sedating of the tricyclic antidepressants. It's sometimes used, along with lithium and Dexedrine, to treat patients who have both manic-depressive disorder and *narcolepsy* (a disorder in which the person keeps falling asleep for brief periods throughout the day).

If the depression doesn't lift in response to the above

treatments, we can try treating it with one of another class of antidepressants—the MAO (monoamine oxidase) inhibitors.

Since another antidepressant, amoxapine (Asendin) blocks dopamine receptors like a neuroleptic suppressing hallucinations and delusions—"crazy thoughts"—it may be particularly effective in psychotic depression.

WHEN LITHIUM IS NOT ENOUGH: THE MAO INHIBITORS

Some psychiatrists believe that MAO inhibitors, such as isocarboxazid (Marplan), phenelzine (Nardil), tranylcypromine (Parnate) and pargyline (Eutonyl), are the most effective antidepressants for bipolar patients, particularly older patients. To date, however, no controlled studies have borne this out.

MAO inhibitor medication works on all three of the important "mood" neurotransmitters: dopamine, norepinephrine, and serotonin. By blocking the enzyme (monoamine oxidase) that destroys these neurotransmitters, it increases their availability.

MAO inhibitors have been used as antidepressants for several decades. Their main drawback is the possibility of a massive release of norepinephrine—with a consequent rapid rise in blood pressure, possibly leading to stroke—if the patient swallows a food, drink, or medicine containing the amino acid *tyramine*.

For this reason, a patient taking an MAO inhibitor must avoid all of the following: aged, dried, or smoked meats and cheeses; yogurt; pickled herring; red wine, beer, coffee, and excessive amounts of chocolate; and cough-and-cold remedies, including nasal sprays. An MAO inhibitor is not ideal for a manic-depressive person who tends to be careless and irresponsible about diet and medication. Nor can an MAO inhibitor be given to a patient taking the antidepressant fluoxetine (Prozac); this combination can lead to a dangerous, possibly life-threatening accumulation of serotonin. Furthermore, only experts should combine tricyclic antidepressants or stimulants with MAOI'S in patients who are resistant to any of these medications alone.

WHEN LITHIUM IS NOT ENOUGH: THE NEWEST REMEDIES

Bupropion (Wellbutrin), a new medication, received FDA approval for marketing beginning in the summer of 1989. Research results suggest that this is an effective antidepressant that does not cause sedation or weight gain. Over the past eight years, we have been directly involved in a clinical study of patients who had frequent periods of mania and who were not helped by lithium and/or antipsychotics. Wellbutrin stabilized mood in 30 percent of these people—a dramatic effect, considering that prior treatments had failed!

Tryptophan and *tyrosine*, two amino acids found in many foods, have recently been found helpful in the treatment of manic-depressive disorders. Tryptophan occurs naturally in milk, meat, fish, turkey, cottage cheese, bananas, peanuts, and all protein-rich foods. The body uses it, along with vitamin B-6, niacin, and magnesium, to produce serotonin. Supplemental tryptophan may help the body produce more serotonin, and thus alleviate depressions caused by low serotonin levels.

Tyrosine, another essential amino acid, comes from phenylalanine and plays a role in the production of dopamine and norpinephine. Some medication-resistant depressions may lift when tyrosine is taken along with the antidepressant.

Patients taking tryptophan or tyrosine must increase their intake of Vitamin B-6, which aids in the production of dopamine and norepinephrine, otherwise the human body may degrade these amino acids into toxic products.

LAPSE AND RELAPSE

Medical disorders such as high blood pressure, seemingly under control, will occasionally relapse. Virtually all branches of medicine struggle with this problem of *relapse*—and that includes psychiatry.

Why do only some bipolar patients relapse? We don't know. Some doctors attribute relapse to differences in treatment methods. Others say it's a function of the patient's particular kind of biochemical imbalance.

One common cause for relapse is too short a course of medication. After the patient has recovered from all symptoms of depression, he still needs antidepressant medication for anywhere from six months to one year. If his medication is discontinued earlier than that, or if the dosage is set too low, there is a 50 percent chance his symptoms will return within a few months.

Seventy to eighty percent of patients who see a psychiatrist for a mood disorder, and who are given appropriate mood-altering medication, experience dramatic relief in four to six weeks. The other 20-30 percent should not lose hope. We rarely give up, as long as the patient is willing to work with us.

Besides changes in medication, and new combinations of medications, hope exists in the form of investigational drugs— medications currently not available by prescription on the American market, but which the FDA has approved for strictly regulated testing at certain research centers. North

Hills Hospital and the University of Kansas Medical School are such centers. At various locations throughout the country, test studies are open to patients who meet the enrollment criteria.

Currently we are studying azamianserin (Mepirzepine) and sustained release adinazolam (Deracyn) for depression. Past studies have focused on buspirone (Buspar), bupropion (Wellbutrin), adinazolam (Deracyn), and alprazolam (Xanax).

All investigational medications must pass animal and human safety tests before they may be tried on patients. Some medications under investigation in the USA are already available by prescription in Canada, Europe, and Japan, such as clomipramine (Anafranil) for obsessive compulsive disorder. If you have a treatment-resistant disorder, you may want to ask your therapist about a medical center near you that conducts investigational drug studies.

Back to the question of relapse, there's a major culprit we haven't mentioned yet: the patient who quits taking his medicine.

PATIENT NONCOMPLIANCE

When we feel pain, we want treatment, and we want it fast. But when our symptoms abate, our commitment to treatment waivers. It's generally agreed that high blood pressure is a harmful condition, yet an estimated 50 percent of people with high blood pressure do not take, or have stopped taking, medication for it. Why? Because high blood pressure causes no symptoms—you can't feel it and you can't see it. Even if a doctor tells you about the risks involved, you may refuse or forget to take your medication because you don't feel sick. High blood pressure is only one of many illnesses for which patients neglect their treatment.

A friend told us about a recent conversation with his mother, who suffers from acute gout attacks:

"Hi, Mom, how're you doing?"

"Well, not too good. My arthritis has been acting up again."

"I thought you said you were feeling better lately?"

"Yes, well, I'd been feeling good, so I figured I didn't need the pills and diet anymore."

Pause. "Let me get this straight. You were feeling bad, so you took the pills the doctor prescribed, and then you felt better." Pause . . . "And then you stopped taking the pills? Mom, that doesn't make any sense. No wonder you're feeling bad again."

Manic-depressive disorder is similar. When the condition is controlled by medication, the symptoms disappear. It's common for patients to forget how bad they felt before treatment. They get negligent about taking their pills, they soon relapse, and then they claim the medication didn't help. That's because they expected it to *cure* their disorder, the way penicillin cures a strep throat. They didn't understand the difference between cure and *control*.

In a cure, the underlying cause is eliminated—the streptococcus bacilli that cause strep throat are actually killed. In mere control, the medication compensates for or counteracts the causes of an illness, but doesn't eliminate them. When control is gone, the illness simply picks up where it left off.

So far, we can control the causes of depression and bipolar disorder, but we don't know how to eliminate them. The patient may need lifelong maintenance treatment—lithium for bipolar disorder—or repeated intermittent treatment with medication for recurrent depression.

Some bipolar patients, with their mood stabilized, may occasionally yearn for the "good old" manic periods. They may even decide on their own to stop taking their medication.

It's a continuing challenge to keep manic-depressive patients compliant with their medication regimen. Some will go off medication once or twice during their lives, and suffer unpleasant consequences. It may take several recurrences of their illness before the lesson sinks in. The better the patient understands the nature of his disorder and the need for continuing medication, the more hope there is for compliance.

THE CRUCIAL DIFFERENCE

Let's review a few facts. A patient doesn't need just any medication; he needs the right medication. Not only does he need the right medication, he needs it in the right amount. And not only does he need the right amount, he needs it at the right time of day.

Yet all these "rights" don't amount to anything at all if he doesn't *take* his medication. That's the crux of the compliance problem.

Here is the real difference between poor and good care. It is not enough that a doctor hands you a prescription for the right medication, the right dosage, and the right times to take it—period. He has to take time to establish rapport with you, educate you, and secure your compliance. He may involve your family, use educational tools, and work with auxiliary staff—including nurses, social workers, and psychologists—to increase the likelihood that you'll take, and continue to take, your medicine. It's the doctor-patient relationship, not the pill alone, that heals.

Chapter 8

Tools for Special Cases

A few psychiatric conditions complicate the treatment of bipolar disorder, as we'll see in the following sections.

RAPID CYCLERS

Rapid cyclers are manic-depressive patients who have at least four episodes of their illness per year. However, many of them are on a nonstop roller coaster. Jacqueline, whom you met in Chapter One, is one of these.

What causes rapid cycling? According to one theory, a certain section of the brain in such patients is vulnerable to nerve cell hyperactivity—the type that occurs in seizures (convulsions). In a process called *kindling*, excitation of the neurons in this particular area then spreads like a brush fire into other brain areas. Eventually there is widespread brain hyperactivity, which causes a burst of manic behavior. Then follows a period of relative neuronal silence, associated with a depressive episode. This ignition–spread–recovery cycle occurs over and over again, resulting in continual manic-depressive episodes.

Because rapid cyclers may take six months or more to reach mood stability on lithium alone, we usually start them on a combination of lithium and the anticonvulsant medication carbamazepine (Tegretol). The rationale is that carbamazepine will calm the hyperexcitable brain cells, as it does in patients with seizure disorders, and thus abort the kindling process.

Of course, it's essential that the patient takes medication regularly. Jacqueline, from Chapter One, wasn't sure she wanted to comply.

"Look, it's simple, I'm spelling it out for you, okay?" she fumed. "I've got a high-pressure job and I'm trying to raise two brats. What the hell do you think you're doing? I've got fifty things to do today, and I'm supposed to take this shit and slow down? No way, Jose! I've got better things to do. I'm feeling more energetic than I have in a month, and I'll be damned if I'm gonna let this stuff drag me down."

When Jacqueline was manic, we had trouble convincing her she'd function better with the medication. And when she was so depressed she could barely get out of bed, she saw no hope for the future—and no reason to bother taking pills. Jacqueline was a tough customer. Eventually, though, she discovered for herself the value of sticking to her medication schedule.

SELF-MEDICATION WITH ALCOHOL
AND STREET DRUGS

"Damn it, I feel like shit. Hung over again. I really don't need this. Work today? No way. Christ, look at

MANIC-DEPRESSIVE OR BORDERLINE?

It's easy to confuse both rapid cyclers and cyclothymic patients (whose mood swings are milder but just as frequent) with people suffering from *borderline personality disorder*. DSM-III-R, the diagnostic manual of psychiatry, says that "the characteristic symptoms of a hypomanic episode, such as less need for sleep, and racing thoughts, are rarely present" in borderline personality. But that's not much of a guide to the clinician who needs to assure proper diagnosis and treatment.

Characteristic "borderline personality" behavior might well be seen in someone with an atypical bipolar disorder. The "borderline" person, who may have had inadequate parenting, lives with a chronic fear of rejection; using manipulative tactics and suicide threats, alternately clinging to others and driving them away. What's confusing is that some manic-depressive people also act this way, presumably to compensate for their frequent, unpredictable mood shifts. The recommended treatment for borderline personality disorder is a combination of intensive insight-oriented psychotherapy, lithium, perhaps low-dose antipsychotic medication, and behavior modification therapy.

Dr. Hagop S. Akisal, who studied 100 patients diagnosed as having borderline personality disorder, found that 45 of them had an unrecognized bipolar disorder. In most cases, the manic-depressive disorder would have been detected if the treating physician had taken a more careful family history. These patients quickly stabilized once they began taking lithium.

me, look at this apartment. It stinks. I stink too. This booze is killing me. I need help.

God, I used to hate this stuff, pour it into the ice bucket, $50 wine and I could throw it away. And now? Now I'm buying bottle after bottle, playing big shot. Now I'm sucking the cork—hell, I'd drink aftershave to get my kicks."

Bruce, 29, is a successful investment banker. He finished high school but never went to college—he was too eager to get out into the work field. School was too slow; he "couldn't stand those idiots." He started as a clerk and worked his way to the top.

Five years ago he began drinking to calm his nerves. At first only at bedtime, and starting at lunch on weekends. A year ago he started having drinks every day after work, to unwind from the day's tension. He stopped at a bar on the way home, and left loaded. The next morning he'd be hung over and irritable—and so edgy that he needed a drink in the morning, "just so I could stomach those jerks at the office." Bruce's life deteriorated. His wife insisted on a separation, and his boss threatened to fire him unless he straightened out.

Faced with the prospect of losing both his marriage and his job, Bruce went to the company's employee assistance program. That's how he came to North Hills Hospital, where he was found to have bipolar disorder complicated by substance abuse.

Over the years, we've seen patients with manic-depressive disorder using alcohol, street drugs, and sometimes both to alleviate their mood swings; tranquilizers, marijuana, or alcohol to calm down from a high; cocaine or amphetamines to fight depression and to keep working at the feverish pace of a manic mood.

A large proportion of manic-depressive patients have alcoholism in their family tree. Research suggests that bipolar disorder, unipolar depressive disorder, and alcoholism are genetically related in some way. Be that as it may, attempts to "self-medicate" with drinks or pills almost always makes manic-depressive symptoms worse and may even render lifetime treatment ineffective.

LITHIUM FOR ALCOHOLISM?

Clinicians have discovered that manic-depressive patients treated with lithium tend to lose their "need" for alcohol or drugs. Some physicians have even suggested giving lithium to treat alcoholics or drug addicts who have no underlying manic-depressive disorder. However, this approach has not been established empirically.

When a heavy abuser of alcohol or drugs has a manic-depressive condition, lithium may control his mood swings, but by itself it probably won't have much effect on his chemical dependency. This type of patient needs the support of a complete rehabilitation program.

PANIC

Recently I received a call from a colleague who asked me to see Sammi, a bipolar patient who continued to have manic "outbursts" despite treatment with lithium and carbamazepine. During our initial evaluation, Sammi indeed described periods of mania followed by depression. However, the fenfluramine diagnostic test suggested a possible complication. We asked Sammi to describe one of her manic "bursts" in detail.

"Sometimes," she said, "I am overwhelmed by my high

periods—it's like someone throws a switch. Three weeks ago I was standing in line at a supermarket, and boom—the mania hit. I got chest pains, I couldn't breathe. I felt like I had to get out of there or I was going to die.

I was so goddamn tense—I was taking lithium at the time, and it obviously wasn't working. So I called my doctor up and told him that I was still feeling high, that the medication wasn't worth a damn. He increased the dosage and said to give it more time—but I still get these bursts of highs."

I asked Sammi if her highs were always so intense—if she always felt she couldn't breathe.

"Yes, they start out of the blue," she said. "All of a sudden I feel terrible."

The mystery of why Sammi failed to respond to lithium and carbamazepine was solved. She had bipolar disorder, all right, but in addition she suffered from *panic disorder*—a condition marked by short periods of intense anxiety. Sammi had been confusing her panic attacks with manic highs, using the same term to describe both conditions. This mixup in terminology had misled her psychiatrist, who diagnosed bipolar disorder but missed the panic disorder.

It is a small percentage of manic-depressive patients who have panic disorder as well. Like Sammi, these patients can be difficult to treat. For one thing, many of them have fears or phobias associated with their panic attacks; often they are afraid of taking pills. Some may find it impossible to leave home, even for treatment; the idea of hospitalization terrifies them.

While the cause of panic disorder is unknown, a panic attack itself is thought to be associated with a sudden excessive release of norepinephrine. The largest group of norepinephrine-producing nerve cells is found in an area of the brain called the *locus ceruleus*. Positron emission tomography (PET) scans of patients having panic attacks show an abnormally high level of activity in the right temporal lobe of the brain—which lends added support to the theory that some people have a physical vulnerability to the development of panic attacks.

Chemical stimulation of cells in the locus ceruleus causes symptoms of panic: sweating, chest pain, dizziness, shortness of breath, and a sense of impending doom. Panic attacks last approximately 15 to 30 minutes, but sometimes the strain exhausts the patient for the rest of the day. The short-term intensity of a panic attack is different from anything seen in mania.

Like Sammi, some manic-depressive patients who also have panic attacks cannot initially differentiate between mania and panic. To them, hypomania feels like an "anxious high"—they're very alert and active, but they feel strangely doomed.

These patients *can* be helped. Medications that blunt the brain's sensitivity to norepinephrine are often effective. Some patients are best treated with a combination of lithium and valproic acid (Depakote) or alprazolam (Xanax). Tricyclic antidepressants and MAO inhibitors may cause hypomania, even though they often help patients who have "pure" panic disorder (i.e., not a combination of panic and bipolar disorders).

Since Sammi panicked during the fenfluramine diagnostic test, we decided to treat her with the recently approved antidepressant fluoxetine (Prozac), which modifies the function of the serotonin system. Sure enough, she did well on a combination of lithium and fluoxetine.

By contrast, a bipolar patient who panics during the Dexedrine challenge test is likely to respond well to a tricyclic antidepressant. When first treated, such a patient may experience anxiety or even hypomania from the sudden overload of norepinephrine (the tricyclic antidepressant prevents the reuptake of norepinephrine into the neurons of the locus ceruleus). However, the overstimulated neurons soon shut off their own receptors and become insensitive to norepinephrine in a process called *down regulation*. Once shut off, these neurons apparently do *not* resume working even in response to a shortage of norepinephrine. This desensitization to norepinephrine prevents panic and anxiety.

If antidepressant therapy is discontinued after six months to a year, approximately 80 percent of these patients appear to remain panic-free, with their mood swings controlled by lithium therapy alone. However, more follow-up studies are needed to confirm this clinical impression.

Chapter 9

Layers of Treatment

Since a psychiatrist is a physician, his primary concern is the patient's physical well-being. When he sees a new patient, he first tries to determine his medical status—are any physical problems causing or contributing to the psychiatric symptoms he reports? He sees the patient's potential problems in four layers:

1. Medical disorders
2. Major psychiatric disorders
3. Residual difficulties
4. Unrealized potential

LAYER ONE: TREATING MEDICAL DISORDERS

As a physician, the psychiatrist fears misdiagnosis. If his patient has a brain tumor or a disorder of the endocrine glands, for example, it would be ludicrous to give her medication for a mood disorder. His first task, therefore, is to find out if she has any medical problem that might be mimicking a psychiatric condition.

"How can I help you?" I ask Ann, my new patient.

Trembling, Ann gets up from her chair and says, "Doctor, I'm a nervous wreck. Look how my hands shake. I can't sleep at night. Everything upsets me. And I can't stand the weather now that it's warming up again—I'm always hot and sweaty. My husband tells me I just have to calm down. But I can't do it. I can't seem to relax."

I ask Ann to sit back down so that I can examine her thyroid gland. Feeling her neck with my fingertips, I ask her to swallow. I feel a node right in front of her throat, and then another node. I take out my reflex hammer. Ann has overactive reflexes: her limbs swing out briskly when I tap the tendons of her joints.

"Before we go any further, Ann," I say, "I'd like to order some thyroid tests. You may be hyperthyroid. Let's take first things first. If you do have a medical disorder, we'll treat it, and then see whether you still feel tense and nervous."

In fact, Ann did have an overactive thyroid gland, secreting too much thyroid hormone T_3 and our endocrinological consultant treated her with antithyroid medication, and her nervousness and tension melted away. Ann's "psychiatric" problem had been purely endocrinological.

INSIDE THE ROLLER COASTER: PHYLLIS

Another patient, Phyllis, also had thyroid-related psychiatric symptoms, but hers were caused by an underactive thyroid.

"Do you believe it? I swear to God I don't believe it,"

Phyllis exclaimed. "All along, the reason I had been feeling rotten was my thyroid, not my lifestyle!

"I was newly married and we had just moved to Michigan. It should have been the happiest time of my life. I'd never felt so loved, so wanted.

"Yet I got to a point where I had almost no energy. I was listless and irritable. I'd never been that edgy before. Every goddamn doctor I went to said it was natural: marriage, a new town, a career change. Two doctors tested my thyroid, all right, but all they did was the simple blood test.

Finally I went to a psychiatrist who injected a releasing hormone and found out I had an increased response. It's like a miracle! I take a simple pill, and I feel *right* about myself. Funny thing—my bowels are regular now, too. I'd been constipated ever since childhood, and I always figured that's just the way I was. Now I find out that was due to the thyroid problem, too."

THYROID MALFUNCTION

In his book *The Good News About Depression,* Dr. Mark S. Gold wrote that if he could perform only one test after screening a patient for alcohol and drug abuse, it would be the thyrotropin-releasing hormone (TRH) stimulation test. He says, "You will find that ten to fifteen percent of the patients you think are depressed have one form or another of thyroid disease, and you wouldn't have found it otherwise. Thyroid dysfunction is the single most important area of misdiagnosis for a mood disorder."

THYROID DISORDERS

There are two broad categories of thyroid malfunction; *hypothyroidism* and *hyperthyroidism*. In hypothyroidism the thyroid secretes too little hormone, slowing down metabolism and causing symptoms almost identical to those found in major depression. In hyperthyroidism the thyroid secretes too much hormone, making the person sleepless, restless, anxious, and explosive— symptoms one would find in a mild manic state.

Although many psychiatrists look for thyroid disease, they may miss subtle malfunctions if they only perform a routine blood test for T_3, T_4 and TSH.

THE TRH STIMULATION TEST IN THYROID DISORDER

Phyllis had found a psychiatrist who performed an additional test for thyroid malfunction—the thyrotropin-releasing hormone stimulation test.

If a patient suffering from subclinical hypothyroidism receives an injection of thyrotropin-releasing hormone (TRH), the blood concentration of thyroid-stimulating hormone (TSH) increases abnormally. That's what happened in Phyllis' case; the test revealed her underactive-thyroid condition to be diagnosed even though a standard blood test had shown her thyroid hormone level to be "normal." It's estimated that in the United States alone, as many as 10 million people suffer from undiagnosed thyroid deficiency that makes them tired or depressed.

Had Phyllis been suffering from a hyperthyroid (overactive

thyroid) condition, it could not have been diagnosed quite that quickly. In hyperthyroidism, the thyroid has already been pushed to work much harder than normal. If TRH is injected, there will be little change from the baseline TSH levels, since the thyroid was already producing as much TSH as it could.

Approximately 40 percent of depressed patients respond sluggishly to an injection of TRH. This blunted response could indicate one of two conditions: hyperthyroidism or major depression. As many as 25 percent of depressed people have the same response to this test as people with hyperthyroid conditions. Thus, the physician has to look at yet another variable: the blood concentration of T4 thyroid hormone. Hyperthyroidism causes an abnormally high T4 level, but major depression does not.

LAYER TWO: TREATING THE MAJOR PSYCHIATRIC DISORDERS

When the psychiatrist is sure that any medical disorders are under control, he focuses on the major psychiatric disorders, including major depressive disorder and bipolar disorder.

OUTPATIENT TREATMENT

Four out of five patients who seek help for manic-depressive disorder can be treated successfully as outpatients. Usually the only patients who need to be hospitalized are those who are suicidal, violent, disruptive, or non-compliant with out-patient treatment.

Outpatient treatment often begins with the diagnostic tests

described in Chapter Six—a process that may take two or three sessions on different days. If the diagnosis is bipolar disorder, your psychiatrist will want to see you every week or every other week during the first two or three months. This allows him to monitor your symptoms and your medication dosage closely.

Once he has the mood disorder stabilized with medication, he can stretch out your appointments to once a month. If you experience no problems between the monthly visits, then appointments can be scheduled every three to six months. We find it's best to see patients at least every six months. Even patients with completely stabilized mood disorders usually require maintenance medication, and the dosage level, especially for lithium, should be checked by a blood test every six to twelve months.

Once-a-year appointments are only recommended for patients who are experienced with their illness, and very stable. We remind these patients to call the moment they notice any minor fluctuations in mood or energy level.

INPATIENT TREATMENT

Roughly 20 percent of patients with manic-depressive disorder require hospitalization within the first month of treatment, because they had a rapid onset or didn't consult a psychiatrist until their problems had become severe.

Obviously, patients who are suicidal, violent, disruptive, uncooperative or exploited by others should be hospitalized. Others may require hospitalization because their rapid, severe mood swings distort their awareness that they have a problem. Hospitalization allows the psychiatrist to monitor such patients closely and design an effective plan for later outpatient maintenance treatment.

We have found that every year, about 15 percent of chronic bipolar patients who are enrolled in outpatient treatment need to be hospitalized. It may be that a patient has not taken his medication as prescribed, or the dosage of medication was too low. But when the patient began having symptoms, neither he nor his family recognized what was happening. Many complications are preventable once a patient develops awareness of his own biological rhythms.

LAYER THREE: RESIDUAL PROBLEMS

The roller coaster ride is over. The car comes to a halt gradually, not suddenly as you feared it might. The attendant, thank God, has the good sense to ease things to a stop. You try to reorient yourself as the attendant walks alongside the cars, unlocking the clamps. The woman ahead of you leaps out as soon as she is freed. You wish you could do the same, but you can't. Nervously you wait as the clamp is loosened, and then you struggle to get up, bracing your hands against the seat. The attendant notices you, extends a hand, and steadies you as you climb out. You're grateful for his help. For a split second, as you're standing there, you don't want to let go.

Everyone with mood swings is apprehensive about getting off the *biochemical* roller coaster and into treatment. Some people eagerly get on with their lives as soon as their moods stabilize. Others need a helping hand.

Fortunately, there's more than one attendant to help you get off this roller coaster. Let's look at different "attendants" bipolar patients can call upon. In addition to the medications described in Chapter Seven, a different kind of help is available.

PSYCHOTHERAPY: PLAYING EMOTIONAL CATCH-UP

"Harvey's taking his medication, but he's at it again," his wife Arlene complains on the phone. "One of the boys asked him a question, and Harvey brushed him off just the way he used to do when he was hyper. I thought that wasn't supposed to happen anymore. I hope you haven't been misleading me about how well he's doing. All I know is, I can't take this much longer."

Mrs. K. tells me, "Sharon spent the whole weekend moping around the house again. You told us the medication would make it easier for her to go out and make friends, but it doesn't seem to be working. She's stopped crying, but all she ever does is sit around the house. For a pretty twenty-year-old girl, that doesn't seem normal."

Harvey's and Sharon's treatments worked—at least physically. Their mood swings stabilized on medication, their sleep improved, and their outlook on life was positive again. But neither of them had managed to adjust psychologically to a healthy state. During their manic or depressive episodes, they had developed what psychiatrists and psychologists call "maladaptive" thoughts and behaviors—known to their families as "acting weird" or "acting up again."

For example, during a manic phase they felt omnipotent and acted irritable and inconsiderate; during a depressed period they felt helpless, hopeless, and unable to do the simplest tasks. Neither the manic nor the depressed thoughts and actions represented their "true selves." But even with their periods of mania and depression under control, Harvey and Sharon did not automatically develop new coping styles. Their maladaptive behavior was outlasting its original biological base. We see this happening in about 10 to 20 percent of bipolar patients, especially those whose mood disorder has lingered for a long time.

HARVEY

Before starting medication, Harvey had seen a psychotherapist for five years. During that time, he was told that the reason he screamed at his children was his unresolved hatred of his own father. Supposedly, if he could overcome his childhood conflicts, he would treat his children better. But no matter how hard Harvey tried, he just couldn't control himself. When the children squabbled, Harvey would fight to control his temper, and finally explode in a rage. The children grew quiet and fearful around their father and tried to avoid him. Finally, when the tension had become unbearable, Arlene gave Harvey an ultimatum: get better help for his emotional problems, or she would take the children and leave. That's when Harvey switched to a different psychotherapist. This clinically well-trained psychologist recognized Harvey's psychiatric disorder, and promptly referred him to us.

Harvey is different now that lithium has smoothed out his emotional roller coaster. He's able to tolerate his children's arguments without flying into a rage. He's no longer in danger of exploding over minor annoyances. But there's still a problem: neither he nor his family trusts the new Harvey. The family still acts as if he's going to blow up at the slightest provocation. Remember, they endured his explosive temper for years. Even though the medication worked within a month, Harvey's *and his family's* everyday behavior patterns are still in operation.

What Harvey needs most right now is *behavior therapy* to help him learn a new set of responses. It's not healthy for him to try to suppress any negative feelings he might have. Instead, he needs encouragement to express his wishes in an assertive, constructive manner. Simultaneously, *cognitive therapy* will help Harvey see himself not as a tyrannical father who can't tolerate his children, but as a man who's in control of his emotions and actions. These two forms of psychotherapy, which focus on specific behaviors and perceptions, can be very effective.

Also, Harvey's wife and children need to understand that neither they nor Harvey's parents are to blame for Harvey's problems. They need counseling about the nature of his problem, the effects of his lithium treatment, and the possibilities for a happier life now that he's off the roller coaster.

Patients like Harvey are often referred to us by family physicians, social workers, and psychologists in the Kansas City area who recognize a need for medication therapy. Performing psychiatric diagnostic tests, prescribing medication, and checking and rechecking dosages is beyond the expertise of many health care professionals. While we are monitoring a patient's medications, we may refer him back to his original therapist for follow-up care such as behavior and cognitive therapy, insight-oriented psychotherapy, or social work.

Lithium helped Harvey, but his wife was initially suspicious. "This isn't the real Harvey," Arlene said to me, "it's just a drugged Harvey. I don't believe people can change their true nature."

Arlene was voicing a common concern. A bipolar patient's family members usually think of him as naturally wild, tempermental, or just "bad," and they initially assume that his medication acts as a kind of chemical straightjacket. They fail to appreciate that what makes a manic-depressive person "bipolar" is a sickness—a neurochemical imbalance in the brain. In fact, *it's the sickness that has been acting as a straightjacket,* strapping their relative against his will into a roller coaster. By restoring the lost balance of brain chemicals, the proper medication unshackles him and sets him free.

SHARON

"Look," I told Sharon, "here are your recent test results. Judging by these results and by the talks we've had, I feel confident that your mood swings have stabilized. There's no reason you can't enjoy yourself. You don't need to lie around the house all day long—that's not what you wanted from treatment. This coming Saturday, I want you to go out and do something you enjoy. Maybe you'd like to go shopping with a friend."

Sharon protested quickly. "But I, I don't . . . I'm afraid to . . . What if . . ."

"What if you become manic again?"

Sharon nodded. "Shopping used to set me off. I'd go out to buy a pair of shoes, then I'd buy a new outfit to go with the shoes, then I'd get a new purse to go with the new outfit. Then I'd decide that I needed *two* new outfits, *two* purses, *two* pairs of shoes . . . I could run up a three-thousand-dollar charge on my credit card in no time at all. Sometimes when I got home I wouldn't even unpack the stuff. I was in a fog. It felt like I was watching someone else go through this incredible spree. But it was me all right—when I got the bill the next month, I knew it was me. What will happen to me if I do that again?"

"Well," I said, "remember that your disorder has been controlled for some time now. By this time, you're clearly in command. It's time for you to realize this and enjoy it. But as a precaution, I want you to take only fifty dollars with you, and no credit cards. Go with a friend, and ask her to help you shop within your means. You can take my phone number with you, and call me if you feel yourself starting to slip, Okay? Come back and see me next week, and we'll talk about how it went. Now, do you agree to do this?"

Sharon nodded yes. Sure enough, she returned to my

office the next week with a triumphant smile. "See, Doc? New shoes with my same old outfit. Don't you love it? And I had enough money left over to treat my friend to a movie and popcorn."

Sharon's symptoms were under control, but she lacked vitality. Our job wasn't finished until her life reflected her improved ability to function. We decided to apply behavior therapy. Working with Sharon, we helped her develop a schedule of activities that included a return to playing tennis and taking dance lessons. Our social worker helped her set up a budget that covered necessities and some affordable extras. We taught her to set goals and follow a plan, instead of making spur-of-the-moment decisions based on her daily moods. Sharon needed a little extra encouragement, and some firm guidance, to help her confront her doubts and get her life moving again. Gradually she started to feel better about herself. Behavior therapy worked for her—because her mood disorder was under control with medication.

LAYER FOUR: UNREALIZED POTENTIAL

Psychiatrists want more for their patients than simple relief from psychiatric symptoms. Our treatment goal is to help a patient live up to his human potential. It's a question of philosophy, but it's also a practical issue.

Former President Jimmy Carter said it well in his book *Why Not the Best?* (Nashville: Broadman Press, 1975). We want every patient to live up to his potential, to undertake what's written into the American Constitution: "the pursuit of happiness." This means we'd like our patients to push themselves to their highest level of functioning—as a benefit to themselves, their families, and the society they live in and serve.

Meet 20-year-old Ken.

"In school, the teachers always told us Ken was such a bright kid," his mother says. "But gradually something went very wrong. He got moody, he stopped going for haircuts, he kept his room like a pigsty, he smoked a lot of marijuana, and he dropped out of school. Sometimes he'd get involved and excited in something, like playing his guitar very loud all night. One evening he came home with his whole body tattooed. We had no explanation for the way he was acting, and we couldn't control him.

"They asked us to get him back into school, but Ken wouldn't go. No matter how upset we got, or how hard we tried to reason with him, he always said, 'F—k school, f—k college. My school is the real world.

"He started to work in the construction business, helping his older brother. He was good at it, his brother said, but he never stuck to a job. Yet in spite of all his turmoil, he always managed to make enough money to survive."

After a thorough examination, we diagnosed Ken as manic-depressive and started him on lithium treatment. Suddenly his life came together.

"It's unbelievable," his mother said. "Ken hasn't been this calm and organized since he was twelve years old. I wonder if he'd have gone through all that pot smoking and wild living if he'd started taking lithium earlier."

"Let's think about his future now," we suggested. "Let's test his IQ, his interests, and his aptitudes." The results confirmed what his mother had told us: Ken's IQ was 129—nearly 30 points above average.

"The sky is the limit," we told Ken. "What do you want to do with your life?"

"Now you're the one who's getting manic, Doc," Ken said with a grin. "You got a little streak of this disorder yourself?"

"Seriously, Ken, it's time to get your act together and move on. What do you see in your future?"

"College," Ken said promptly. "I think I'll go for a double major—English and business."

A year later, Ken sent me a heartwarming postcard from St. Louis: "I haven't reached the sky yet, but I'm up here above the clouds—a scholarship and the dean's list at Washington University. Mood swings no longer rule my life."

When a patient reaches the point where he is symptom-free, he and his psychiatrist can move on to consider his lifestyle and how it might change for the better. Together, they can devise a treatment strategy that will help him realize his full potential. *The ultimate goal of treatment is growth. This means not just freedom from symptoms, but life lived to its fullest potential.*

We've had patients tell us, "I just want to be normal." But what is normal? Some "normal" people are very energetic, some are calmer. Some are happiest curling up with a good book; others want and need to push themselves to the limit. A patient should think about his own inner needs, and discuss them with his psychiatrist.

One of the most rewarding aspects of psychiatric practice is to work with someone who has lost his ability to function, and to help him regain control over his life and then reach goals he has set for himself.

HELPING HANDS

Psychotherapy can be very effective, once the biological malfunction of manic-depressive disorder is controlled. Medication gives the patient relief from symptoms, but it does not teach attitudes and actions that should replace symptom-riddled behavior.

Succinctly: *all* patients with a severe biochemical imbalance that causes bipolar disorder need treatment to correct the imbalance. That job is best done by a biologically oriented psychiatrist. Some patients will require psychotherapy or psychological counseling after their symptoms are gone, in order to live normal or fuller lives. That layer of treatment is often best handled by a social worker, psychologist, or psychotherapist working along with the psychiatrist.

Dr. Frederick K. Goodwin in "Depression and Manic-Depressive Illness" quotes one of his patients who described the necessity for a balance between medication and psychotherapy: "Pills cannot, do not, ease one back into reality. They bring you back headlong, careening, and faster than can be endured at times. Psychotherapy is a sanctuary, it is a battleground, it is where I have come to believe that I someday may be able to contend with all of this. No pill can help me deal with the problem of not wanting to take pills, but no amount of psychotherapy alone can prevent my manias and depressions. I need both."

EARLY DETECTION AND SELF-REFERRAL

At this point, you're becoming an informed consumer. You've learned to recognize many of the danger signs of bipolar illness, as described in Chapter Two. You understand—intellectually if not emotionally—that a mood disorder is no one's "fault." If you're manic or depressed, perhaps you're no longer blaming yourself for your inability to control your emotions; perhaps you've stopped blaming your parents for causing your problems. Ideally, you have accepted the idea that bipolar disorder is caused by a biochemical imbalance that's outside your control. And we truly hope you realize that you need not be a slave to this disorder.

By now, you've learned that this condition can be corrected. In reading this book, in wanting to learn more about bipolar disorder, you're already halfway across the threshold.

Chapter 10

Life Without the Roller Coaster

"I've been wide awake at five A.M. every day for the past week. I think I might be headed for trouble again. Maybe I'd better set up an appointment."

—Harvey

"Last night I couldn't sleep, so I got up and wrote ten letters. God, I had to go to the post office to get another package of stamps this afternoon. I've been doing that a lot lately."

—David

When a patient begins treatment, I often ask him to rate his moods on the Beck scale (see Chapter Two) twice a day, and to keep a record of his behavior. Recordkeeping increases a patient's sensitivity to his own moods and actions. Soon, patterns may emerge: during a manic episode, one patient may spend hours on the telephone, another may gamble or drink excessively; during a depressed period, he may lose his appetite and shed pounds, or overeat, or start to drink more, or avoid leaving the house. Most patients can learn to identify their feelings and patterns of behavior, and recognize them as warning signs of either manic or depressed periods. At North Hills Hospital, we teach this mood awareness.

It's crucial to the patient's long-term health that he notify his psychiatrist promptly at the first recognition of warning signs. The patient, his family, and his psychiatrist work as a team to manage the illness. As long as the partnership functions smoothly, the effects of the illness can be overcome.

AVOIDING THE ROLLER COASTER RIDE

"Last weekend, my boss invited me and my husband to a fancy corporate dinner—a really big deal. Normally I might turn down something like this, but this time I had to go. Well, everything was going Okay. I had just one glass of wine before dinner, nothing more. But then during dinner there was this real lull in the conversation. I could feel people getting bored. I started to get nervous—what if they were bored with me? I thought, If I weren't here I bet they'd be having a great time. It's my fault. I have to do something quick to get things going. I started to call the waiter over for a Scotch and water. Then it hit me. Here you go again: another drink, then your voice gets louder, you start telling wild stories, even dirty jokes. Anything to get the ball rolling. The real life of the party. I remembered our sessions. I caught myself switching into high gear. I realized I wasn't a boring person—this was just a boring dinner. It wasn't my fault that these people acted bored, and it wasn't my job to entertain them. I told the waiter to bring me decaf. No more Scotch, no more life of the party. No more roller coaster rides."—Jacqueline

As a result of her treatment for manic-depressive illness, Jacqueline has learned to interpret an impulse to act up as a possible warning sign of mania. She recognized her vulnerability, and she was able to catch herself before she crossed the line, took one drink too many, and acted inappropriately. Jacqueline now knows that if she loses her judgment, gets drunk, skips her lithium dose, and starts thinking she can do without "these damned pills," she may be in for another bumpy ride.

Bipolar patients who are taking medication for their illness should think of themselves as recovering from an emotional disorder. Continuing recovery depends on taking the medication regularly. Many stressful situations can magnify a mild hypomanic episode that's still under control by medication. Thus, it's important to keep stress to a minimum.

"Sure, I know enough not to go to the racetrack, or drink, or even shop when I'm feeling high," another patient tells us. "But I can't go through life without ever entering a mall or going to a place where drinks are served. What should I do?"

The following steps may help patients stay off the roller coaster:

Step 1: Follow your doctor's directions. Take your medication as prescribed, and see your physician regularly. If you slip or feel yourself losing control, call the doctor immediately. Don't wait for the disorder to wreck your life.

Step 2: Resist impulsivity. No matter what you're doing, think twice, three times before following a whim. When shopping, plan your excursions; make a list and stick to it. Avoid those last-minute, "I have to run down to the store and pick up a————" situations. Leave your credit cards at home, and just take enough cash to buy what you need. Know your limits.

Step 3: Don't hide it. Tell your spouse or a close friend about your disorder. Make certain this person is aware of your problem. If you need his or her support, ask for it.

Step 4: Reach out. Join a support group for people with manic-depressive disorder. Many such groups now exist. In "mood-swinger clubs," as they're sometimes called in Kansas City, the group serves as a magnifying glass, enlarging and clarifying the problem all its members share. A patient may steadfastly refuse to see certain problems in himself until he sees the same problems in others. The self-help group can help you resist the temptations of mania-provoking situations, and encourage you to stay on your treatment regimen. To find a support group in your area contact:

National Depressive and Manic-Depressive Association
222 South Riverside Plaza
Suite 2812
Chicago, Illinois 60606
(312) 993-0066

Step 5: Remember the past, but don't relive it. As strange as it may seem, patients may long for the highs of their roller coaster days. They associate their manic periods with vitality, fun, and a feeling of omnipotence. For some patients, this selective memory can be seductive: "Remember the time I worked for four days straight?" "How about that crazy night with the girls? Man, I was really something then." The temptation can be so strong that the patient drops out of treatment, mistakenly trying to move from remembering the past to reliving it.

But the psychiatrist will bring the patient back to reality by challenging his nostalgia: "Was it really 'fun' when you destroyed the family's finances—when you almost ruined your marriage? In retrospect, do you admire the way you treated your children—and yourself? Was that fun? And how about the depression that followed, was that fun, too?" A sobering splash of reality can dampen those longings for "the good old days." It's important for patients to remember the past—both the good *and* the bad.

With a thorough knowledge of their disorder, and with the treatment approaches outlined in this book, bipolar patients can gain control over their lives off the roller coaster.

We began this book with Jacqueline's experience of what life on a roller coaster is like. Listen to her now.

J: "I bet he'll ask me what I thought about when I was driving up here," I thought. And sure enough, Doc, you did.

MD: "Okay, let's hear about it."

J: "I looked at my watch. It was five o'clock, and I had a whole hour for just a forty-minute ride to your place during rush hour. Believe me, that hasn't happened before. I had actually twenty minutes more than I needed. You know, I don't run out of time any more . . . (pause).

"It's amazing, it's a paradox! I get everything done and there's still time. My husband is so patient. Could it be that he isn't pushing me anymore? No—he's the same old Dennis. The peace is within *me*.

"You know, I think I even breathe slower. It's wonderful. I have time to smell the roses, as they say.

"As I drove up here, there was even space between the cars. It was still rush hour, but I didn't feel rushed. I never noticed the space before. I always drove bumper to bumper.

"There's not just space between the cars, there are periods between my thoughts nowadays. I seem to see things from above. I look down and see all the bustling, and I know what's important.

"You said a manic-depressive rides through life on a roller coaster, blindfolded, not knowing whether she will go up or down, not able to drop the blindfold or stop the ride. I'm riding it, all right, but there's no blindfold any more and I have my foot on the pedal. It's my own ride, not my roller coaster's ride.

"God Himself must have invented lithium, either after he created man or after he nearly destroyed him in the big flood. It's as if he knew about the ups of creation and the downs of destruction."

MD (jokingly): Are you sure you're all right, Jacqueline, or are you getting onto a religious kick now? Maybe we'd better check your lithium level! See you next week.

J: Same time, same place.

SOURCES

Akiskal, Hagop S., "The Milder Spectrum of Bipolar Disorders: Diagnostic, Characterologic, And Pharmacologic Aspects," *Psychiatric Annals*, 17:1 (January 1987), pp. 32–37.

———; Hirschfeld, Robert M. A., and Yerevanian, Boghos I., "The Relationship of Personality to Affective Disorders," *Arch. Gen. Psychiatry*, 40:7 (July 1983), pp. 801–10.

American Psychiatric Association, *Diagnostic and Statistical Manual of Mental Disorders*, 3rd edition, revised. Washington: American Psychiatric Association Press, 1987.

Baldessarini, Ross J., *Biomedical Aspects of Depression*. Washington: American Psychiatric Association Press, 1983.

Baron, Miron, and Rainer, John D., "Molecular Genetics and Human Disease," *British Journal of Psychiatry*, vol. 152 (1988), pp. 741–53.

Beck, A.T., et al., "An Inventory for Measuring Depression," *Arch. Gen. Psychiatry*, vol. 4 (1961), 561–71.

Blehar, Mary C.; Weissman, Myrna M.; Gershon, Elliot S., and Hirschfeld, Robert M.A., "Family and Genetic Studies of Affective Disorders," *Arch. Gen. Psychiatry,* 45:3 (March 1988), pp. 289–92.

Cadoret, Remi J., "Evidence for Genetic Inheritance of Primary Affective Disorder in Adoptees," *Am. J. Psychiatry* 1135:4 (April 1978), pp. 463–66.

Carlson, Gabrielle A., and Kashani, Javad H., "Manic Symptoms in a Non-Referred Adolescent Population," *Journal of Affective Disorders,* vol. 15 (1988), pp. 219–26.

Coryell, William, "Outcome and Family Studies of Bipolar II Depression," *Psychiatric Annals* 17:1 (January 1987), pp. 28–31.

Dunner, David L., "Stability of Bipolar II Affective Disorder," *Psychiatric Annals* 17:1 (January 1987), pp. 18–19.

Egeland, Janice A., interview, "New Findings on the Heritability of Bipolar Disorder," *Currents,* 6:6 (June 1987).

Fieve, Ronald R., *Moodswing: The Third Revolution in Psychiatry.* New York: Bantam Books, 1975.

Freud, S. 1952-1955. *Gesammelte Werke Chronologisch Geordnet,* Bd. 1-17. London: Imago Publishing.

Gershon, Elliot S.; DeLisi, Lynne E.; Hamovit, Joel; Nurnberger, John I., Jr; Maxwell, M. Elizabeth; Schreiber, Judith; Dauphinais, Deborah; Dingman, Charles W. II, and Guroff, Judith J., "A Controlled Family Study of Chronic Psychoses," *Arch. Gen. Psychiatry,* 45:4 (April 1988), pp. 328–36.

————; Hamovit, Joel; Guroff, Juliet J.; Dibble, Eleanor; Leckman, James F.; Sceery, Walter; Targum, Steven D.; Nurnberger, John I.; Goldin, Lynn R., and Bunney, William E., Jr., "A Family Study of Schizoaffective, Bipolar I, Bipolar II, Unipolar, and Normal Control Probands," *Arch. Gen. Psychiatry,* 39:10 (October 1982), pp. 1157–67.

Gold, Mark S., *The Good News About Panic, Anxiety, and*

Phobias. New York: Villard Books, 1989.

————, *The Good News About Depression*. New York: Villard Books, 1986.

————; Lydiard, R. Bruce, and Carman, John S., *Advances in Psychopharmacology: Predicting and Improving Treatment Response*. Boca Raton, FL. CRC Press, 1984.

Gold, Philip W.; Goodwin, Frederick K., and Chrousos, George P., "Clinical and Biochemical Manifestations of Depression," *New England Journal of Medicine*, 319: 6 (August 11, 1988), pp. 348–53.

————; Goodwin, Frederick K., and Chrousos, George P., "Clinical and Biochemical Manifestations of Depression. Part 2," *New England Journal of Medicine*, 319: (August 18, 1988), pp. 413–20.

Goldman, Daniel, "Pioneering Studies Find Surprisingly High Rate of Mental Ills in Young," *New York Times*, January 10, 1989, page C1.

Goodwin, D. W., *Alcohol and the Writer: An American Epidemic*. Kansas City and New York: Andrew and McMeel, 1988.

Goodwin, Donald W., and Guze, Samuel B., "Affective Disorders." In *Psychiatric Diagnosis*, (4th edition). New York and London: Oxford University Press, 1989, pp. 3–42.

Goodwin, Frederick K., "Depression and Manic-Depressive Illness," National Institute of Mental Health Publication #82-1940, 1982.

Griesinger, W., *Mental Pathology and Therapeutics*. New York: William Wood and Co., 1882.

Guide to the New Medicines of the Mind, edited by Berlant, Jeffrey; Exten, Irl, and Kirstein, Larry. Summit, New Jersey: PIA Press, 1988.

Hammen, Constance; Adrian, Cheri; Gordon, David; Burge, Dorli; Jaenicke, Carol, and Hiroto, Donald; "Children of Depressed Mothers: Maternal Strain and Symptom Predictors of Dysfunction," *Journal of Abnormal Psychology* 96:3, (1987), pp. 190–98.

Hershman, J. D., and Lieb, J., *The Key to Genius*. Buffalo, N.Y.: Prometheus Books, 1988.

Holzman, Philip S.; Kringlen, Einar; Matthysse, Steven; Flanagan, Steven D.; Lipton, Richard B.; Cramer, Gunnar; Levin, Smadar; Lange, Kenneth, and Levy, Deborah L., "A Single Dominant Gene Can Account for Eye Tracking Dysfunctions and Schizophrenia in Offspring of Discordant Twins," *Arch. Gen. Psychiatry* 45:7 (July 1988), pp. 6341–47.

Keeler, Linda L., and Othmer, Ekkehard, "Atypical Bipolar Disorder: Is it a Distinct Entity?" *Psychiatric Annals*, 17:1 (January 1987), pp. 21–27.

Klerman, Gerald L., "The Classification of Bipolar Disorders," *Psychiatric Annals*, 17:1 (January 1987), pp. 13–17.

Kline, Nathan S., *From Sad to Glad*. New York: Bantam Books, 1974.

Konner, Melvin, "New Keys To The Mind," *New York Times*, July 17, 1988, pp. 49-50.

Jefferson, J.W.; Greist, J.H.; Ackerman, D.C.; and Carroll, J.A., *Lithium Encyclopedia for Clinical Practice* (2nd ed.), Washington: American Psychiatric Press, 1987.

Little, K.Y., "Amphetamine, But Not Methylphenidate, Predicts Antidepressant Efficacy," *Journal of Clinical Psychopharmacology*, 8:3 (June 1988), pp. 177–83.

Ludwig, Arnold M., *Principles of Clinical Psychiatry*. New York: Grune & Stratton, 1985.

Meeks, John E., *High Times/Low Times*. Summit, New Jersey: PIA Press, 1988.

Mindell, Earl, *New and Revised Vitamin Bible*. New York: Warner Books, 1985.

Mitterauer, B.; Leibetseder, M.; Pritz, W.F., and Sorgo, G. "Comparisons of Psychopathological Phenomena of 422

Manic-Depressive Patients with Suicide-Positive and Suicide-Negative Family History," *Acta Psychiatr. Scand*. Vol. 77 (1988), 436–42.

Othmer, E.; Penick, E.C.; Powell, B.J.; Read, M., and Othmer, S.C., *The Psychiatric Diagnostic Interview*, revision by E.C. Perrick. Los Angeles: Western Psychological Services, 1989.

Othmer, Ekkehard, and Othmer, Sieglinde, *The Clinical Interview Using DSM-III-R*. Washington: American Psychiatric Association Press, 1989.

Othmer, Ekkehard; Penick, Elizabeth C., and Powell, Barbara J., *Psychiatric Diagnostic Interview Manual*. Los Angeles: Western Psychological Services, 1981.

Ramsey, T.A.; Frazer, A.; Mendels, J., and Dyson, W.L., "The Erythrocyte Lithium-Plasma Lithium Ratio in Patients with Primary Affective Disorder," *Archives of General Psychiatry*, vol. 36 (April 1979), pp. 457–61.

Ryan, Neal D., and Puig-Antich, Joaquim, "Affective Illness in Adolescence." In *American Psychiatric Association Annual Review*, vol. 5. Washington; American Psychiatric Association Press, 1986, pp. 420–50.

Strober, Michael; Morrell, Wendy; Burroughs, Jane; Lampert, Carlyn; Danforth, Holly, and Freeman, Roberta, "A Family Study of Bipolar I Disorder in Adolescence," *Journal of Affective Disorders*, vol. 15 (1988), pp. 255–68.

Targum, S., and Marshall, L.E., "Fenfluramine Provocation of Anxiety in Patients with Panic Disorder," *Psychiatric Research*, in press, 1989.

Targum, Steven D., and Gershon, Elliot S., "Pregnancy, Genetic Counseling, and the Major Psychiatric Disorders." In *Genetic Diseases in Pregnancy*. New York: Academic Press, 1981.

Weisberg, Lynne W., and Greenberg, R., *When Acting Out Isn't Acting: Understanding Child and Adolescent Temper,*

Anger and Behavior Disorders. Summit, New Jersey: PIA Press, 1988.

Weissman, Myrna M.; Gershon, Elliot S.; Kidd, Kenneth K.; Prusoff, Brigitte A.; Leckman, James F.; Dibble, Eleanor; Hamovit, Joel; Thompson, Douglas; Pauls, David L., and Guroff, Juliet J., "Psychiatric Disorders in the Relatives of Probands With Affective Disorders," *Arch. Gen. Psychiatry*, 41:1 (January 1984), pp. 13–21.

Weissman, Myrna M.; Gammon, Davis; John, Karen; Merikangas, Kathleen R.; Warner, Virginia; Prusoff, Brigitte A., and Sholomaskas, Diane, "Children of Depressed Parents," *Arch. Gen. Psychiatry*, 44:10 (October 1987), pp. 847–53.

Zahn-Waxler, Carolyn; McKnew, Donald H.; Cummings, E. Mark; Davenport, Yolande, and Radke-Yarrow, Marian, "Problem Behaviors and Peer Interactions of Young Children with a Manic-Depressive Parent," *Am. J. Psychiatry*, 141:2 (February, 1984), pp. 236–40.

Zahn-Waxler, Carolyn; Mayfield, Anne; Radke-Yarrow, Marian; McKnew, Donald H.; Cytryn, Leon, and Davenport, Yolande B., "A Follow-Up Investigation of Offspring of Parents With Bipolar Disorder" *Am. J. Psychiatry*, 145:3 pp. 506–09.

INDEX

ABOUT THE AUTHORS

Ekkehard Othmer, M.D., Ph.D., Professor of Psychiatry at the University of Kansas Medical Center and Medical Director at North Hills Hospital of Kansas City, Missouri, a member of Psychiatric Institutes of America (PIA). Dr. Othmer is a Diplomate of the American Board of Psychiatry and Neurology and one of its examiners; he is also a fellow of the American Psychiatric Association and a member of the American Medical Association, Society for Neuroscience, American Association for the Psychophysiological Studies of Sleep, Psychiatric Research Society, Society of Biological Psychiatry, and other organizations. Dr. Othmer graduated from the Department of Psychology (Ph.D.) and the Medical School (M.D.) of the University of Hamburg and trained in psychoanalysis at the Psychoanalytic Institute in Hamburg, West Germany. He completed his residency in psychiatry at Renard Hospital, Washington University Medical School, in St. Louis, Missouri.

Sieglinde C. Othmer, Ph.D., is Research Assistant Professor of Psychiatry at the University of Kansas Medical Center, where she is conducting psychotropic investigational drug studies. She is a member of the Society for Clinical Trials and of the Affiliate Staff of Research Psychiatric Center in Kansas City, Missouri. She is the mother of three children. Dr. Othmer studied Romance languages at the Sorbonne in Paris, France, and graduated from the Social Sciences Department of the University of Hamburg, West Germany. She completed a postdoctoral fellowship in genetics at Renard Hospital, Department of Psychiatry at Washington University, in St. Louis, Missouri.